W9-AWP-439

Intellectual Property Protection

Intellectual Property Protection

What Engineers and Other Inventors Need to Know

Third Edition

Virginia Shaw Medlen, J.D.

PROFESSIONAL PUBLICATIONS, INC.
BELMONT, CA

INTELLECTUAL PROPERTY PROTECTION
What Engineers and Other Inventors Need to Know
Third Edition

Printed in the United States of America

Professional Publications, Inc.
1250 Fifth Avenue, Belmont, CA 94002
(650) 593-9119
www.ppi2pass.com

Current printing of this edition: 1

Library of Congress Cataloging-in-Publication Data
Medlen, Virginia Shaw.
    Intellectual property protection: what engineers and other inventors need to know /
Virginia Shaw Medlen.--3rd ed.
    p. cm.
    Rev. ed. of: Intellectual property protection / David S. Goldstein, Virginia Shaw
Medlen. 2nd ed. c1992.
    Includes bibliographical references and index.
    ISBN 1-888577-46-0
    1. Intellectual property--United States. 2. Engineers--United States--Handbooks,
manuals, etc. I. Goldstein, David S. Intellectual property protection. II. Title.

KF2980 .G65 2000
346.7304'8'02462--dc21   99-047208

TABLE OF CONTENTS

PROFESSIONAL PUBLICATIONS, INC.

PREFACE

This book is meant to be a guide for engineers, inventors, high-tech entrepreneurs, and other business professionals who want to protect their intellectual property. While it is designed to provide accurate and authoritative information, it is not a substitute for legal advice or expert assistance. This is because the law, like life, is constantly evolving. Unless you keep up with the changes (and few of the professionals with whom I am acquainted have the time for such a task), you will need to consult with a professional who does.

This new edition has been rewritten and updated in response to the significant changes that have occurred since the last printing. Government fees, as you might expect, have changed. Last year, fees actually went down for the first time in the history of the U.S. Patent Office. While the fees included in the appendix are current as of this printing, they will certainly change. Before paying any fee, be sure to check with the appropriate government agency, or check with your intellectual property attorney to make certain that you pay the correct amount.

Substantive changes have also occurred in the federal laws affecting patents and copyrights. The Sonny Bono Copyright Term Extension Act of 1998 has extended the life of most existing copyrights by an additional 20 years. More important, the incredible expansion of the internet has created new challenges for owners of patents, trademarks, and copyrights, and new risks for web site owners and internet service providers. At least some of these risks have been addressed by Congress in the Digital Millenium Copyright Act. In a radical change of direction, the U.S. Patent Office has acknowledged that software can be patented, offering software developers stronger protection than that traditionally available through the copyright laws.

The right of employers to the intellectual property created by their employees, or by independent contractors hired by them for that purpose, continues to be a minefield for the unwary, as does the protection of trade secrets. As two engineers formerly employed by a large Texas firm recently found out after years of litigation and appeals following a criminal conviction, a departing employee should always ask before taking anything from his or her employer that might be a trade secret or other kind of intellectual property.

Intellectual property litigation continues to be a relatively expensive affair. This, more than any other reason, is why the services of a competent intellectual property attorney should be sought as soon as possible if you are at all uncertain of your rights to intellectual property or unsure of how best to protect your intellectual property. In the law, as in medicine, prevention is always cheaper than a cure.

Virginia Shaw Medlen, J.D.
San Francisco, CA

PROFESSIONAL PUBLICATIONS, INC.

ABOUT THE AUTHOR

Virginia S. Medlen is a 1985 graduate of the Southern Methodist University School of Law. She is admitted to practice before the U.S. Patent and Trademark Office, the state bars of California and Texas, and numerous federal courts, including the U.S. Supreme Court. She is a member of the American Bar Association, the American Intellectual Property Law Association, and the International Trademark Association. Elected as a Life Fellow of the Texas Bar Foundation, Virginia has also been honored by inclusion in "Who's Who in American Law." As a former Texas Instruments manufacturing engineer, she understands the special problems faced by engineers in high-tech industries. As a partner in the San Francisco office of the intellectual property law firm of Medlen & Carroll, LLP, Ms. Medlen assists clients in acquiring, licensing, and protecting patents, trademarks, trade secrets, copyrights, and mask works.

INTRODUCTION

An engineer's job requires creativity. So it is likely that during your career as an engineer you will invent or write something. You also might design a symbol or trademark. These works are examples of intellectual property. The types of intellectual property you might want to protect include the following:

- literary works

- drawings

- computer software

- audiotapes

- films and records

- trademarks and trade names

- trade secrets

- semiconductor chips, including read-only memory chips (ROMs), and the mask works used to produce them

- inventions

USING THE LAW AND LAWYERS

Creating intellectual property requires time and effort. It is only fair that you benefit from your effort. Ownership of intellectual property gives you certain rights. However, it is up to you to protect your work from unauthorized use. This book will tell you how.

Of course, the safest way to protect something is to lock it up and never use it or show it to anyone. That will rarely be to your advantage, however. The next safest plan is to protect your intellectual property by carefully applying the law.

Constitutional basis. Laws protecting intellectual property derive their authority from Article I, Section 8 of the U.S. Constitution.

> The Congress shall have power... to promote the progress of science and useful arts, by securing for limited times to authors and inventors the exclusive right to their respective writings and discoveries.

Do you need a lawyer? You might be surprised how easy Congress has made it in some cases to protect your own work. It might be simply a matter of filing the proper forms and paying a recording or application fee. In some cases, however, it might be necessary to hire an attorney who specializes in intellectual property protection.

Some works, such as books, can be protected without the assistance of a lawyer. Other types of intellectual property require expert attention almost from the beginning. The need for a lawyer early in the process is especially important if you want to protect an invention. Having a lawyer conduct a patent search at an early stage might save you from reinventing something already patented.

If you have intellectual property rights that you feel are being infringed, you probably will need a lawyer to handle your case. You cannot easily fight an infringement case without an attorney.

Otherwise, the decision to seek legal counsel is up to you. Be sure to take into consideration the complexity of the application process for your kind of intellectual property. For instance, assuring copyright protection for an article you have written for a trade journal will require simply affixing the appropriate copyright notice to the work. Registering the copyright with the federal government will require only filling out a form and paying a small fee. Patenting an invention will be more difficult.

COPYRIGHTS

Literary works constitute one of the best-known forms of intellectual property and perhaps are the simplest to protect. These include published and unpublished fiction and nonfiction such as textbooks, reference works, directories, catalogs, advertising copy, compilations of information, drawings and other designs, photographs, mask works, and computer programs. Other works that can be protected by copyright include musical scores; musical performances captured on records, audiotapes, compact discs, and the like; motion pictures captured on film, video tape, DVD, and the like; and sculpture, paintings, and other fine works of art. These and other nondramatic works can be protected simply by affixing the appropriate copyright notice to the work. You can register the copyright with the federal government. (The specific application forms for protecting periodicals and serials differ slightly. The forms for protecting dramatic works also differ, but they are not discussed here.)

WHO CAN CLAIM THE COPYRIGHT

The copyright is used to protect virtually anything you might write. Generally speaking, you can claim a copyright if you are the author of a work, and you can claim a copyright in that part of a collaborative effort that you wrote. If the collaborative work cannot be split into separately authored sections, then all authors can claim a copyright in the whole work.

Works-made-for-hire. According to the law, the author is not always the person who did the writing. In some situations, the author can be the employer of the person who created the work, or the person who commissioned the work from an independent contractor. For example, an employee who writes something for his employer is not the author of the writing: the employer is. A work-made-for-hire is defined by the law as:

- a work prepared by an employee within the scope of employment

- a work specially ordered or commissioned, if the parties expressly agree in a written agreement made in advance of the creation of the work that the work shall be considered a work-made-for-hire, and if the work is

  — a contribution to a collective work

  — a part of a motion picture or other audiovisual work

  — a translation

  — a supplementary work

  — a compilation

  — an instructional text

  — a test

  — answer material for a test

  — an atlas

Other works cannot be works-made-for-hire. Agreements made before the creation of works not listed above, or after the creation of any work, can affect ownership, but cannot affect authorship of the work.

REGISTERING YOUR COPYRIGHT

A copyright arises upon the creation of the work. If, however, you wish to enforce your copyright, you must first register the copyright. Because statutory damages and attorneys' fees often cannot be awarded for pre-registration infringement, prompt registration of both published and unpublished works is generally preferred.

You can register your copyright by filing the proper form with the U.S. Copyright Office, located in the Library of Congress in Washington, D.C. If your work has been published, you need to submit two copies of it (each bearing the appropriate copyright notice) with the application. If it has not been published, only one is needed. You also must include a fee.[1]

Publication. To the Copyright Office, publication means the distribution of copies of a work on a nonconfidential basis to anyone, such as to the public by sale, rental, lease, or lending. It does not require that the work be professionally printed and bound.

---

[1]A fee schedule appears in Appendix B.

Fixed and tangible form. To be considered published, your work must also meet the fixed and tangible form requirement. This stipulates that the work must be in permanent form, such as in print or on a recording. You cannot consider an impromptu speech to be published unless you write it down, and you cannot consider a song or musical piece to be published unless you produce it as sheet music or as a recording. Therefore, you cannot register copyrights in these intangible forms of intellectual property.

Registering your copyright with the Copyright Office is straightforward. You can get the proper forms, which are free, by requesting the type and quantity of forms you need from the Copyright Office's Information and Publication Section.[2] You also can call the Copyright Office to request forms, or download and print the forms from the Copyright Office's website.

Forms. The Copyright Office publishes different forms for different categories of copyrightable material.

- Form TX, for nondramatic literary works

- Form VA, for works of visual art, such as illustrations, drawings, or photographs

- Form GR/CP, to be used with Form TX or VA, for a group of works you are contributing to periodicals

- Form PA for works of performing arts, including musical works, dramatic works, motion pictures, and audio-visual works

- Form SR for sound recordings fixed after February 15, 1972

You must use form RE to renew a copyright registration granted while the 1909 Copyright Act was in effect (prior to January 1, 1978). You need form CA to correct or supplement a previously filed form.

All of these forms can be ordered by mail from the Copyright Office (see the address shown in Appendix A) or, if you have access to the internet, they can be downloaded from the Copyright Office's website (also shown in Appendix A).

Expedited registration. If one of your previously unregistered works needs to be registered quickly (e.g., if litigation or a contract are pending), you can expedite the registration. This requires a letter from an attorney certifying that you

---

[2] Important addresses and phone numbers are listed in Appendix A.

require and are eligible for an expedited registration. If qualified, your work will be registered within five working days. This action requires an additional fee.

CORRECTING ERRORS

Under the 1909 copyright law (works created prior to January 1, 1978), errors in the copyright process often resulted in loss of copyright protection. Failure to deposit a copy of a work meant loss of protection, as did using an improper copyright notice.

Under the 1976 copyright law (affecting works created between January 1, 1978 and March 1, 1989), however, the penalties for mistakes are less severe. You need only to file Form CA with the Copyright Office, with the proper fee, to correct or amplify the original registration. Time is of the essence, however. Leaving an incomplete, incorrect, or improper copyright notice or registration for too long might diminish your protection. You are excused for making omissions on a relatively small number of copies, but, because this standard is vague, your best bet is to correct the error as best and as quickly as you can. Some copyright notice defects made prior to March 1, 1989, may not be correctable.

TERM OF PROTECTION

The new copyright law changed the term of the protection given by copyrights. The term thus depends on whether the work was copyrighted while the old law was in effect, or after.

Under the 1976 and 1989 Copyright Acts. Works that are created on or after January 1, 1978 are protected automatically and immediately upon creation.[3] If created in portions at different times, each portion of a work is protected immediately upon its completion.

Generally, copyright protection lasts for the author's life plus 70 years. If more than one person collaborated on a work, the term extends 70 years beyond the last surviving author's death.

Works-made-for-hire and works whose authors do not identify themselves to the Copyright Office are protected for 95 years from the date of publication or 120 years from the date of creation, whichever occurs first.

---

[3] The Copyright Act of 1976 became effective January 1, 1978.

Under the old law. The term of protection differs for works copyrighted before January 1, 1978. Under the 1909 law, copyright protection became effective on the date the work was published, or, if the work was unpublished, on the date of registration.[4] Protection lasts 28 years from the date it was secured. The copyright is renewable in the last (28th) year of its first term. The new Sonny Bono Copyright Extension Act (1998) extends the renewal term of copyrights secured before 1978 to 67 years, making the total protection term 95 years.

Works copyrighted in other countries. Works created in a country that is a signatory to any copyright treaty with the United States are protected in the United States. Following the Copyright Restoration Act, many foreign works that had fallen into the public domain for failure to comply with U.S. rules on marking, registration, and renewal have had their copyright protection restored. Under the present rules, if the copyright in a foreign work is enforceable in the country of creation, then it is enforceable in the United States. There are some exceptions in the Act for the protection of persons and companies in the United States who used or reproduced these works in the United States prior to the enactment of the Act.

RENEWALS

To process extended renewals for works copyrighted before 1978, the Copyright Office requires Form RE. The Copyright Office does not need another copy of the work. Failure to file for renewal during the year in which a pre-1978 copyright expires permanently forfeits protection beyond the year of expiration. For example, a work copyrighted in 1973 would be eligible for renewal in 2000. Because the new copyright law extends the renewal term to 67 years, a renewed copyright would last until 2067. If the copyright owner fails to file for renewal in 2000, she/he will lose protection forever after that year. Renewals are only required for works originally created in the United States and registered prior to 1978. Renewals are not required for works originally created in another country.

Works that were created before 1978, but were not published or registered, can be simultaneously registered and renewed by submitting the required documents and fees for both. The copyright term will extend to 70 years after the author's death, or until December 31, 2002, whichever comes later. If published before December 31, 2002, the term of the copyright will extend to 70 years after the author's death or until December 31, 2047, whichever comes later.

---

[4] The Copyright Act of 1976 superseded the Copyright Act of 1909.

Who can renew a copyright. Copyright renewals can be claimed by the author or, if the author is deceased, by the author's spouse or children. If a deceased author has no surviving spouse or child, and the author left a will, the executor of the author's estate can renew a copyright. If the author left no will, or if the estate already has been distributed, the appropriate next of kin can renew the copyright.

If a work's copyright owner is not the person who wrote the work, the copyright owner can renew the copyright only under certain conditions. She/he can renew the copyright in a posthumous work, a periodical, a cyclopedic or other composite work, a work copyrighted by a corporation otherwise than as an assignee or licensee of the individual author, or a work copyrighted by an employer for whom the work was made-for-hire.

WHAT CAN BE COPYRIGHTED

There is a critical distinction concerning what you can and cannot copyright. You cannot copyright ideas, concepts, or facts. You can copyright only the original expression of these ideas, concepts, or facts. For example, you cannot copyright the fact that the Dodgers beat the Yankees in 10 innings, but you can copyright a written report describing the game, provided the prose is your own. Similarly, you cannot copyright an idea for a technical journal article you'd like to write, but you can copyright the article once you've written it.

Titles cannot be copyrighted. This does not mean that anyone may freely use the titles of your works. If someone uses your title in order to mislead people into thinking his work is yours, you might have the basis for a lawsuit on the grounds that he is "palming off" his work for yours. But if he does not intend to fool people—say, he simply likes the title and intends to reach a different audience—then you might have no recourse.

Blank forms and other items. You also cannot copyright blank forms, names, short phrases, slogans, lettering, coloring, lists of contents, processes or devices, or works that consist solely of common property, containing no original authorship (e.g., standard calendars, charts, or schedules). However, you can copyright the original, literary text on otherwise uncopyrightable items. Some of these items, such as short phrases, slogans, lettering, and colors, may be protectible as trademarks.

Items in the public domain. You also cannot copyright works in the public domain. These are works that already have been distributed and, for one reason or another, are not protected by a copyright. For instance, a work whose copyright term has expired and has not been renewed enters the public domain and is forever available for any use. Once a work enters the public domain, it stays there, unless the copyright law provides otherwise.

Works that were never copyrighted and are no longer eligible to obtain a copyright also enter the public domain. An anthology or other collective work consisting of an assembly of works in the public domain, however, might be eligible for copyright protection.

If you obtained your copyright registration before January 1, 1978, you must renew your copyright during the one-year period of renewal eligibility to prevent your work from entering the public domain.

Government publications. You may freely extract from government publications when you write. The Copyright Office states, however, that if you publish a work that contains significant material from government publications, your copyright notice should indicate which parts of the work are yours. Your copyright does not cover the portions extracted from government publications.

Misconceptions. Several misconceptions about copyrights exist. One is that a work must be entirely unique to be copyrighted. In fact, you can copyright a work that is similar to another if you did not copy the other work. The courts will decide if your work is too similar to another to be original, if the other author sues you for infringement.

Another misconception is that to protect your work you must register it with the federal government. Actually, you may consider your original work copyrighted the instant you write it. For maximum legal protection, however, you will need to register your copyright.

MISCELLANEOUS WORKS

There are several other types of works that engineers might need to copyright. Each type is handled differently.

Drawings. Drawings and text must be copyrighted separately. You must submit Form VA (used for published or unpublished works of the visual arts) to register your drawings. You need to send Form TX (for published or unpublished non-dramatic literary works) to register your text.

Audiovisual works. Registering audiovisual works is similar to registering literary works. For pictorial, graphic, and sculptural works, use Form VA. For motion pictures and other audiovisual works, use Form PA.

New versions of existing works. A copyright protecting a new version of a previously copyrighted work covers only the new material. The author is the person who created the new material. If the author of the new material is different from the original version's author, only the new author may renew a copyright in that portion of the work.

UNPUBLISHED WORKS

You do not need to publish a work to copyright it. Even an unpublished work is considered copyrighted upon its creation. In fact, you do not even need to publish a work to register it with the Copyright Office. All forms used to register published works also can be used for unpublished ones.

This has not always been the case. Under the 1909 act, a work had to be published to be registered, and the work had to be registered to enable the copyright owner to sue in a federal court for infringement. States had varying degrees of protection for unpublished works, but publication was a prerequisite for federal protection under the 1909 act. The federal act automatically became effective when a work was first published.

The current copyright law extends protection to unpublished works. You might find advantages to registering your unpublished works. The most obvious, of course, is that you have the maximum federal protection. However, registering your work—whether published or unpublished—with the Copyright Office means anyone can gain access to your work and read it. The Privacy Act Advisory Statement found on copyright registration forms says anything you write on that form will be used to establish and maintain a public record. The work you submit with the form is also considered public. Therefore, do not register any work that you do not want the public to read.

If your previously registered, unpublished work gets published, you do not need to reregister the work, but you may do so if you wish. The Copyright Office will need two copies of the published version, should you desire to reregister it.

COPYRIGHT NOTICE

For works created prior to March 1, 1989, the copyright notice requirement is simple but crucial. It indicates to others that your work is copyrighted and that they cannot copy it without your permission. There are three acceptable forms of copyright notice: the word "Copyright," the symbol ©, and the abbreviation "Copyr." All three forms require the year and the name of the copyright owner.

For example, the following three copyright notices result in the same protection in the U.S.

Copyright 1985 John Doe
© 1985 John Doe
Copyr. 1985 John Doe

International notice. While any one of these forms legally protects you in the U.S., only the © form, followed by the sentence, "All rights reserved," offers the maximum international protection.[5] Such a notice would look like this:

© 1985 John Doe. All rights reserved.

Anonymous, pseudonymous, and collaborative registration. If you wish to remain anonymous, you can use a copyright notice like this:

© 1985 Anonymous

It is legal to withhold your name even from the Copyright Office, but to do so limits the copyright term to 95 years from the date of publication. If you remain anonymous on the work itself but reveal your name to the Copyright Office, you are entitled to the usual term ending 70 years following your death.

You also can register your copyright under a pseudonym. The pseudonym would be the name on the copyright notice. The same copyright term limitation applies to a pseudonymous author as to an anonymous one.

For a collaborative work (one that you write with one or more other people), the notice should contain all authors' names. For a collective work (a collection of separate works by different authors), separate notices should be listed together, each containing one author's name, the year he published his part of the work, and the © symbol.

Phonorecords of sound recordings. The form of copyright notice on phonorecords is similar and consists of three elements:

- ℗
- Year of first publication
- Name of the copyright owner

---

[5] The phrase "All rights reserved" protects you in the following countries, which are parties to the Buenos Aires Convention (BAC) of 1910: Argentina, Bolivia, Brazil, Chile, Colombia, Costa Rica, Dominican Republic, Ecuador, Guatemala, Haiti, Honduras, Mexico, Nicaragua, Panama, Paraguay, Peru, and Uruguay.

For works created under the new copyright act (on or after March 1, 1989), copyright notice is not required. However, including a notice in the form described above is still desirable since it prevents an infringer from avoiding actual or statutory damages by claiming innocent infringement.

Registering unpublished works. The copyright notice is unnecessary for unpublished works, but it is a good idea to affix a notice (such as the following) to all copies that leave your hands. This will help avoid unintentional unauthorized publication.

Unpublished Work © 1985 John Doe

Works distributed in pieces. If you wish to protect works that you distribute in pieces, register each piece separately and place a copyright notice on each piece as you distribute it. This applies in cases such as class notes distributed weekly, portions of design plans given to a client over a period of time, and other similarly distributed works.

Items of negligible value. Registering copyrights involves time, effort, and money. In most cases, registration does not require great amounts of any of these, but registering works of little or no value might not be worthwhile.

YOUR RIGHTS

What does a copyright do for you? It gives you the exclusive right to the following:

- To reproduce the copyrighted work
- To prepare derivative works based upon the copyrighted work
- To sell, rent, lease, or lend copies to the public
- To publicly display the copyrighted work

Advantages to registering. Although the 1976 copyright law affords you significant protection without requiring you to register with the Copyright Office, there are several advantages to registering. It publicly establishes your copyright and enables you to sue infringers. Registration also establishes the validity of your copyright if the work is published without a copyright notice, provided the work is registered within five years of publication. Furthermore, registration enables you to collect statutory damages and attorney's fees in addition to actual damages and profits in successful infringement suits, if the work is registered within three months of publication or prior to the infringement.

Registration is a prerequisite to an infringement suit unless the infringed work is a Berne Convention work whose country of origin is not the U.S.; the application, fee, and deposit were delivered to the Copyright Office in proper form and registration was refused; or the infringed work consists of sounds, images, or both, the first fixation of which was made simultaneously with its transmission.

Transferring a copyright. A copyright signifies ownership. Therefore, you may sell, license, trade, or transfer by any other means, the rights to your work. If the copyright is owned jointly, a co-owner may transfer only the portion of the copyright that he owns.

When registration becomes valid. Copyright registration becomes valid on the date the Copyright Office receives everything it needs in acceptable form. The Copyright Office will not send a confirmation that it received your documents, but it will return a self-addressed, postage-paid postcard that indicates the date your application was received, if you enclose the card with your application. It might take three or more months to receive a registration certificate or a rejection and explanation.

WHERE YOU ARE PROTECTED

Copyright protection in the U.S. covers all of your unpublished works, regardless of your nationality and in what country you live. A published work is protected in the U.S. if one or more of the authors is a U.S. citizen or resident on the work's first publication date, or is a citizen or resident of a foreign country that has signed a copyright treaty with the U.S. A work also is protected if it is first published in the U.S. or in a foreign country that is a member of the Universal Copyright Convention (UCC) or the Berne Convention on the first publication date.[6]

---

[6] UCC members are Algeria, Andorra, Argentina, Australia, Austria, Bahamas, Bangladesh, Barbados, Belgium, Belize, Brazil, Bulgaria, Cameroon, Canada, Chile, Colombia, Costa Rica, Cuba, Czechoslovakia, Denmark, Dominican Republic, Ecuador, El Salvador, Fiji, Finland, France, Germany, Ghana, Greece, Guatemala, Guinea, Haiti, Hungary, Iceland, India, Ireland, Israel, Italy, Japan, Kampuchea, Kenya, Laos, Lebanon, Liberia, Liechtenstein, Luxembourg, Malawi, Malta, Mauritius, Mexico, Monaco, Morocco, Netherlands, New Zealand, Nicaragua, Nigeria, Norway, Pakistan, Panama, Paraguay, Peru, Poland, Portugal, Senegal, Spain, Sri Lanka, Sweden, Switzerland, Tunisia, U.K., U.S., U.S.S.R., Vatican City, Venezuela, Yugoslavia, and Zambia.

Foreign protection. Protecting a work in other countries requires a different strategy. Unfortunately, some countries like China, Saudi Arabia, and Iran offer little or no protection for U.S. works. No international copyright exists. However, many countries, including the U.S., belong to the UCC and the Berne Convention, and all member countries agree to honor copyrights granted by all other member countries, as long as each copyrighted work is enforceable in the country in which it was created, and bears the © symbol, the name of the copyright owner, and the year of the work's first publication. In addition, the phrase "All rights reserved," placed after the copyright notice, is required to protect your work in Buenos Aires Convention (BAC) countries.

Also, the U.S. maintains bilateral copyright agreements with some countries. You can obtain a current list from the Copyright Office's Information and Publications Section.

If you are interested in protecting your work in a particular country, you should investigate that country's procedures, if any, for registering and enforcing copyrights. It would be best to do this before your work is published anywhere, because protection often depends on the circumstances surrounding initial publication.

INFRINGEMENT

A copyright gives you exclusive rights to reproduce your work in virtually any format. If someone violates your right, you have cause to sue for infringement. To sue someone you believe is an infringer of your copyright, you will need to register your work and probably will need to hire a lawyer.

Injunctions and restraining orders. As a first step, you can ask the court to issue a temporary injunction or restraining order, but only if your copyright is federally registered. A simple hearing in which you exhibit the copyright registration certificate itself is often all it takes to have the court issue an injunction against further infringement. This injunction will protect you while you are waiting for the case to go to court.

Writ of attachment. If you feel that the defendant is likely to move his assets out of the country to prevent losing them to you in court, you can ask a judge to issue a writ of attachment. This order prevents the defendant from moving his funds until a subsequent trial concludes.

In court. In addition to proving that the defendant copied your work, you also need to prove that you own the copyright. This part is relatively simple, because you must have registered the work in the Copyright Office in order to have initiated the lawsuit. The courts consider registration with the Copyright Office to be sufficient evidence that you own the copyright.

The ease with which you can prove the defendant copied your work depends largely on whether he used your words verbatim or paraphrased your work. The former, of course, is much easier to show. If the latter is the case, you must prove that the defendant had access to your work (which might be tricky, if your work is unpublished), and you must convince the jury that the two works are similar enough that the defendant must have copied your work. The court will evaluate similarity of structure and of expression in determining whether a verdict is warranted in your favor.

Winning the case. If you win the case, the court will issue a judgment against the infringer, preventing him from producing any more copies of the infringing work. The court also might award you actual damages (in an amount that the court believes you have lost because of the infringement) or the profits the infringer made by copying your work.

You have another option if your lawsuit is successful. Instead of accepting actual damages, you can request statutory damages, which allows the judge to decide how much to award you. Ordinarily, statutory damages range from $500 to $20,000 for all infringements of any one work, although for willful infringement the maximum can range up to $100,000. The minimum award for innocent infringement is $200. The amount usually depends on the extent of infringement and on whether or not the infringement was intentional. You might also collect attorney's fees in addition to statutory damages. You cannot collect statutory damages or attorney's fees for infringement that begins before registration of your copyright, except for published works where registration is applied for within three months after the date of first publication.

Fair use. Some uses of a copyrighted work are allowable, however. These fall under the fair use section of the copyright law. This section says that using copyrighted material for criticism, comment, news reporting, teaching (including multiple copies for classroom use), scholarship, or research, does not constitute infringement. The section specifies the criteria by which to judge fair use:

- Was the material used for commercial purposes, or for nonprofit educational purposes?
- What is the nature of the copyrighted work?

- What proportion of the copyrighted work was used?

- How has using the copyrighted material affected its potential market value?

Photocopying. Photocopying all or part of a copyrighted work, unless it is done for one of the purposes considered fair use, is an infringement of copyright. This is one of the most common modes of copyright infringement.

Because photocopying is so widespread, it is equally important to know how to avoid copyright infringement and still get vital information to employees who need it, without having to endure the delays of a lengthy routing list. Here's how:

- Implement a company copying policy; post clear warning signs at all copiers, and include detailed guidelines in your company's employee manual and ethics training.

- If certain publications are widely read by employees, make certain that your company has enough subscriptions to ensure a short routing list.

- Rather than circulating entire articles or publications, try circulating copies of the tables of contents or the first page of each article, and keep the original publications in a central location for easy access to interested employees.

- If copying and circulating entire articles is important to your business, consider obtaining a license from Copyright Clearance Center, a not-for-profit corporation located at 222 Rosewood Drive, Danvers,Massachusetts 01923 (www.copyright.com), which serves as a single-source copyright licensing and royalty collection center for over 8,000 publishers. A blanket license varies in cost depending on the extent and type of photocopying. Alternatively, you can keep a log of copies and pay the appropriate royalty (usually about 50 cents) for each copy.

Book piracy. Unlike most cases of infringement, which involve illegally copying portions of a protected work, book piracy is the reproduction of entire texts. Book piracy takes two primary forms: printed book piracy and unauthorized photocopying. The former is the unauthorized publishing of a book whose copyright belongs to someone else. The latter is the wholesale photocopying of entire works. Both practices are widespread, especially in some Asian and Latin American countries.

American publishers have been trying to curb book piracy, particularly by negotiating with the governments of the countries most often cited as piracy nations.

The publishers have been largely unsuccessful. The main problem is that international law does not consider intellectual property appropriation to be theft.

If you suspect your work is being pirated abroad, you should consult with an experienced copyright attorney to determine whether action can be taken to stop the piracy or to prevent the exportation of pirated copies out of the country of origin.

ENGINEERING WORKS

Engineering works, such as proposals, blueprints, models, and architectural plans, have limited copyright protection. Copyrights protect only the expression of ideas or concepts, not the ideas or concepts themselves. Thus, copyright protects both two-dimensional and three-dimensional works, including drawings, models, and buildings constructed from such drawings prior to December 31, 2002. Rights to the buildings constructed are limited and do not extend to pictures, photographs, or similar likenesses of the buildings. Also, there is no prohibition against subsequent modification or destruction of the buildings.

Thus, protecting the expression is usually the best you can do under copyright law. You can copyright your description and drawing of a product, thereby preventing someone else from exactly copying those works. If someone sees your plans, however, and if he can duplicate the product without actually having a copy of your plans, he may be able to do so if the product is purely utilitarian. A copyright in your writings and illustrations might be sufficient, however, due to the complexity typical of most engineering plans. In these cases, a would-be infringer will be unable to build from your idea without having a copy of your plans.

This presents you with a dilemma. Registering your work with the Copyright Office makes details of the work available to the public, so you should not register anything you want kept secret. On the other hand, if your work is going to be made public by, for example, the publication of a book or the sale of a product, you need to have registered your work in order to sue an infringer.

The best thing to do in such a case probably is to refrain from registering your work, at least until you anticipate widespread distribution. Until you complete the registration process, you might want to rely on nondisclosure agreements with individuals to whom you show your works.[7] Your copyrights are reserved

---

[7] See Appendix D.

upon the works' creation, whether or not you register them. If you do decide to sue someone for infringement, however, you would have to register the work. Registering after the infringement takes place makes you ineligible for statutory damages and attorneys' fees, but at least you can stop the infringement and collect actual damages.

Works made for a client. The law not only protects the works you create for yourself or your company, it also protects works you create as a contractor for a client or other third party. For instance, suppose a client asks you to create plans for constructing a roadway or building. Such plans cannot be a work-made-for-hire because such works are not qualified by the copyright law for that protection. Therefore, unless there is a written agreement assigning ownership of the plans to the client, you (or your company) will retain ownership. While the client may use the plans to build the road or building, it may not copy or modify the plans, or lend, sell, or give the plans to another.

To retain maximum control and rights regarding your work created for a client, you should place the copyright notice on each copy of each document, and get in writing all agreements concerning ownership and disclosure of engineering plans. Place a statement concerning ownership on each document, as well. Some engineers use statements like this:

> The use of these drawings and specifications shall be restricted to the original use for which they were prepared and publication thereof is expressly limited to such use. Reuse, reproduction, or publication by any method, in whole or part, is prohibited without the written consent of the engineer. Title to the designs remains with the engineer without prejudice. Visual contact with these drawings constitutes prima facie evidence of the acceptance of these restrictions.

SOFTWARE

You will encounter special problems if you want to copyright computer programs (software). Protecting computer programs, of course, was beyond the intentions of the authors of the 1909 Copyright Act. Over the years, the courts have struggled with the problem of how software fits into copyright protection. Application of copyright law to software is in a state of flux.

Nevertheless, you can protect your software to a great degree. Much of the process is the same for software as for other literary works. You should, however, be aware of some limitations.

What you can copyright. You can copyright only your program's source code (i.e., what you actually write). You can protect your object code (i.e., the computer-compiled code), the program's function (in some cases), and possibly the name of your program, in ways that are covered elsewhere in this book. You should also be able to protect most software by obtaining a patent.

As with all other forms of literary documents, your program must be original to be copyrighted. For instance, you cannot copyright a simple counting or timing loop that does nothing original.

The same rules concerning what not to copyright, and how to renew copyrights granted before 1978, also apply to software. Also, you must use copyright notice for all works created prior to March 1, 1989.

Registering your program. To register the copyright in a program, you must send Form TX with the proper fee to the Copyright Office. If your program is published, include either a diskette that contains the object code or two copies of the first and last 25 pages of a listing of the source code, if the source code is not a trade secret. (Some experts say you are better protected if you send the entire text, not just the first and last 25 pages, of a program listing that is longer than 50 pages.) The more comments that appear in the source code listing, the easier it probably will be to prove that the program is yours. If you deposit only the program's object code, however, the resulting registration is considered a "risk of doubt" registration because the Copyright Office cannot read object code.

Some experts believe that you actually are protecting the source code by filing a listing of the object code, although this point has not been litigated. The primary reason for registering the object code is that object code almost always is legible only to a computer. This prevents others from reading the copy of your program registered in the Copyright Office.

Source codes. On the other hand, if you do not consider your source code a secret (see Trade Secrets elsewhere in this book), you might wish to register the first and last 25 pages of that code, as well. The Copyright Office does not require a copy of the entire program unless it is less than 50 pages long.

Usually, however, it is best to invoke trade secret status for your source code to prevent anyone from ever seeing it. In this case, you would either not register the source code or petition the copyright office to permit the deposit of only the first and last 10 pages of source code to avoid disclosing trade secrets. If you do not want to register your source code, at least include a copyright notice on any copies of it you might have, especially if you intend to distribute them.

Registration might be unnecessarily risky, particularly if you doubt that a competitor would be able to write a program to do the same thing even if he disassembles your object code—without seeing your source code. In that case, you might want to refrain from registering your program until you think you might need to assert your copyright, if at all.

Copyright notice. It is particularly important that you place the copyright notice on all programs created prior to March 1, 1989. As with other documents, all copies of your source code must bear proper notice. Remember the proper format: either "Copyright," "Copyr.," or the © symbol, plus the year of publication (or of registration if the work is unpublished), and the copyright owner's name. Also remember that, if the work is a work-made-for-hire, the employer owns the copyright. Placing "All rights reserved" with your notice provides the same international protection for software as for other copyrighted material.

You must also place the copyright notice on every diskette that contains your program, and it should appear on the screen every time your program is run. Note that most computers do not have a © symbol. Do not make the mistake of using (C) (a letter C in parentheses) to replace the © copyright symbol. Using (C) alone is the same as excluding a copyright notice, and will forfeit your protection until you correct the omission.

Shrink-wrap laws. Some states have enacted so-called "shrink-wrap" laws, which stipulate that removing the plastic shrink-wrap from a software package constitutes the purchaser's agreement to the conditions of sale displayed on (not in) the package. The conditions usually specify that the purchaser cannot copy in any manner the contents of the package. The validity of shrink-wrap licenses is unclear.

Revisions and derivative works. You should register the copyright in new versions of programs along with programs based on other programs. Even if the changes are slight, registering the copyright in the new versions can help protect them.

Related material. You also should register your user, installation, and troubleshooting manuals, and any descriptive material concerning your program, such as advertising copy and packaging. Do not forget to place copyright notices on these items.

Infringement. Someone can infringe your software copyright in one of two ways. First, he can copy the code, perhaps with the intention of selling it under a different name. Second, he can duplicate the entire program, e.g., from one diskette to another, without your authorization. Once you have registered your copyright, you can take action against both types of infringement.

Catching infringers of your program copyright is usually more difficult than catching someone who infringes your copyright in other types of material. Part of the difficulty is that you might not know who is doing the copying. It is your responsibility to monitor new programs that seem similar in function to yours.

If you know that someone is copying your work, you will probably have more trouble proving infringement than you would if he copied another type of document. Code copiers are especially difficult to stop, because someone judging the similarity of your work and the supposedly copied one cannot look as easily for whole sections and routines copied verbatim. Most likely, a copied version will look significantly different. You might want to insert into your programs some initials, meaningless phrases, or commands that do nothing. If those commands show up in someone else's program that looks similar or performs similarly to yours, you can prove more readily that the work was copied.

Reverse engineering. Reverse engineering of computer programs is entirely legal. You cannot stop someone from studying how your program works, or even disassembling it, and then developing his own program from what he learns.

Screen displays. You might also want to register the screen displays of your particular program. For example, you might not want anyone to copy an original design or sequence that your program creates on the screen. This might seem redundant if you have registered the entire program, but this additional precaution might increase protection.

The more unusual and complex the screen is, the more you will want to protect it. Software art and computer game screens are good examples. You can register static screens by sending Form PA, the filing fee, and photographs of the screens. You can register changing screens by sending Form VA, the filing fee, and a videotape of the screens. Forms PA and VA are for protecting only the screens, however. You still will need Form TX to protect the program. Remember that the copyright notice must appear in the program listing and on the screen.

Not all screens are registrable, however. You cannot register database screens, spreadsheets, business graph generators, or word processing screens, for example.

Reiteration. To reiterate, placing copyright notices on copies of your source code protects you against someone copying the source code. Placing copyright notices on your diskettes and on the screen protects you against someone copying the object code from one diskette to another.

SEMICONDUCTOR CHIP MASK WORKS

Protecting the masks from which semiconductor chips are made has been problematic. Fortunately, legislation has begun to deal with the difficulties.

Semiconductor Chip Act. For years, semiconductor companies and designers, lawyers, judges, and juries have debated the possibility of extending copyright protection to semiconductor chips. The Semiconductor Chip Protection Act, which was meant to reduce legal difficulties arising from mask works, became law in 1984.

What is protected. The Chip Act does not actually grant protection to the chips themselves, but to the images or patterns on the masks from which chips are made. The act protects these elements even though, in contrast with copyright law, they are purely functional, not ornamental.

When protection begins. Protection under the act begins on the date the mask work is registered in the Copyright Office if the mask work already has been exploited commercially. Protection of a mask work registered in the Copyright Office but not yet exploited commercially begins the date of first commercial exploitation anywhere in the world.

Under the Semiconductor Chip Act, the Copyright Office will register a mask only if the design is original, is not a standard in the semiconductor industry, and was first commercially exploited on or after July 1, 1983.[8] Masks first exploited between July 1, 1983 and November 9, 1984 are protected if they were registered before July 1, 1985. All chip masks first exploited before July 1, 1983, and those first exploited after July 1, 1983 and before November 9, 1984, but not registered by July 1, 1985, might be protected by state laws, but are ineligible for federal registration.

In practice, the Copyright Office has applied a "de minimus" standard to reject mask works that appear to be simple designs. For some technologies, such as microwave chip mask works, what appears to be simple is, in fact, a complex design for particular applications. In such cases, an administrative appeal can result in a registration being granted.

---

[8] To exploit a mask work is to distribute chips produced from it to the public for commercial purposes. Distribution includes offering, in writing, to sell or transfer such chips, provided the chip that embodies the mask work already exists.

Chip protection differs from protection of other types of copyrightable works in one particularly important way. You must register your mask work with the Copyright Office within two years of the mask's first commercial use in the U.S. or abroad. Protection is not automatically conferred upon creation.

How to register. To register a mask work, send a completed Form MW, a filing fee, and samples. The sample requirement for commercially exploited works is four chips (dies) as first exploited and one set of reproductions of each mask work layer. The reproductions can be plastic color overlays, composite plots, or photographs of the layers, magnified 20 to 30 times their actual size.

For unexploited mask works, you must submit overlays or composite plots of each layer. You do not need to send the chips themselves.

In cases where such full disclosure is undesirable, you have another option. If filing overlays, plots, or photographs of your mask work's layers would reveal a trade secret, you may withhold reproductions of one or two layers of a mask work that consists of five or more layers. If the work is exploited, send four chips plus a printout reproduced in microfilm of the work's design data pertaining to each withheld layer. Block out or strip the sensitive material from the deposit. If the work is unexploited, send microfilm reproductions with the sensitive material blocked out or stripped, and a photograph of the work's top layer and any other layer visible from a single exposure.

The Copyright Office might grant exceptions to these trade secret requirements for masks. If you feel additional protection is needed, you can petition the Chief of the Examining Division.

Try to register. You should attempt to register any mask that is worth more than the filing fee, even if you believe the Copyright Office will reject it as being too standard or unoriginal. You will need to certify that you at least attempted to register your mask work if you intend to sue someone for infringement.

Copyright notice. Also, unlike other forms of copyrightable material, chip masks do not need to display a copyright notice to be protected. To help avoid unauthorized copying, however, you should affix a notice on the mask or on chips made from the mask. The Copyright Office requires the copyright notice to consist of the owner's name following the words "mask work," the symbol *M* (the letter M preceded and followed by an asterisk), or a Ⓜ symbol (the letter M in a circle). You do not need to include the year. A mask work notice might look like this:

Ⓜ John Doe

Mask work protection is valid for 10 years and is not renewable. This term is shorter for mask works than for other copyrightable works.

Foreign protection. A valuable mask work in the U.S. is likely to be just as valuable in another country. The Chip Act recognizes the potential international market for a good mask. The act established a three-year transition period, ending November 1987, during which foreign individuals could register masks first commercially used outside the U.S., but only if the Secretary of Commerce determined that the country of which the individual is a citizen is taking proper steps toward similar chip protection laws or toward signing a chip treaty with the U.S.

Infringement. You can sue for infringement of a mask only if you are the owner of the work (i.e., its creator or the creator's agent), or if you have been granted all rights to it through transfer or license. You cannot sue someone who infringed more than three years before the suit is brought.

Also, you cannot sue an innocent purchaser of a semiconductor chip product that was copied from your mask. An innocent purchaser is someone who imported or distributed the goods without knowing the mask was copied and who did so before being notified that the goods infringe a protected work. Reasonable grounds to believe a mask is protected constitute notice of protection. An innocent purchaser must pay a royalty, of an amount to be decided in court, on infringing chips he bought prior to receiving notice of protection but imported or distributed after receiving notice. Individuals who buy chips from an innocent purchaser are not liable.

Damages imposed on mask work infringers are similar to those imposed on infringers of other protected works. A court might award the work's owner actual damages and the infringer's profits, or, if the owner requests, the court might grant statutory damages of up to $250,000. The court also will decide whether or not to restrain the infringer from distributing more copied chips, or to order infringing chips to be seized or destroyed.

ROM protection. Whether or not the Chip Act covers read-only memory (ROM) chips remains to be clarified by the government and the courts. Recent cases indicate that ROMs are protected if they meet the same criteria by which other works are judged: They must be original and nonstandard, and they must meet the same manufacturing requirements. Some court cases also have upheld copyright protection for software stored in ROM.

Hardware boards. It also remains unclear whether or not hardware boards are patentable. You clearly can protect the artwork for them, however, by registering copyrights in the drawings.

PATENTS

Patents protect new and useful inventions. They are more complicated, more expensive, and more difficult to obtain than copyrights. Patents also differ from copyrights in that, while ideas are not patentable as such, a well-drafted patent claim will protect the concept of an invention. The U.S. Patent and Trademark Office, located in Arlington, VA, reviews all applications for patents.

TYPES OF PATENTS

The Patent and Trademark Office grants three types of patents:

- Plant patents protect newly developed plants that were produced asexually, such as by grafting or by rooting cuttings. Plant patents are not covered in this book.

- Design patents cover nonobvious, original appearances given to new or existing products.

- Utility patents, the most common type of patents, protect the function of inventions.

UTILITY PATENTS

According to patent law, an invention is a novel and useful idea that has been reduced to practice. Having been reduced to practice means that the idea works or has been described in detail in a patent application.

What can be patented. Not all inventions are patentable, however. To be patentable, an invention must be a useful process, machine, manufacturing method, composition of matter, or a new and useful improvement thereof. The invention must be original. It also must be new, which means it was never known or used by anyone else in the U.S. and was never patented or described in writing

---

anywhere. Also, you must not have received an inventor's certificate or patent in another country for the invention more than a year before you file in the U.S.

Another hurdle is the nebulous nonobviousness requirement. This stipulates that a patent cannot be obtained for an invention or improvement of prior art if the invention or improvement would have been obvious to someone with ordinary skill in the invention's field.

Attorneys. Clearly, the requirements alone for obtaining a patent merit the advice of professional legal counsel. You should hire a patent attorney as early as possible. Patent attorneys have degrees in both law and engineering.

Conducting a patent search. Your attorney can assist you in the patenting process. First, a patent search should be conducted to ensure that the invention has not been patented before. You may wish to begin this process yourself, by going to a patent library or conducting a patent search on the U.S. Patent Office database, which is accessible through the PTO website (see Appendix A). However, as this database only includes patents issued during the last 25 years or so, a more thorough search should be conducted if your initial search does not turn up a bar to patentability of your invention. Your patent attorney can hire a professional patent searcher to conduct a more thorough search. The results of a good patent search will help you decide whether or not your invention can be patented. Although the search results might disappoint you, it is far better to know whether there are any problems before you invest the often significant funds required to prepare and file a patent application. Furthermore, even if the search uncovers "prior art" similar to your invention, you may be able to redesign your invention to be substantially different.

Your attorney should know as much about your invention as possible before he begins your patent application. This will help ensure that your patent, if granted, gives you the broadest possible protection without making the validity of your patent questionable due to claims that are too broad. Your patent might be invalid if your invention does not live up to all of the assertions in your patent application, and such assertions may be used against you if you are sued for personal injury caused by your invention.

The application. Your patent attorney will prepare your application. A well-prepared application describes your invention in sufficient detail for someone skilled in the appropriate field to make and use it. Nevertheless, the language used on the application should be understandable to someone without a technical background. Few judges have engineering degrees, so avoid overly technical language wherever possible.

A patent application typically consists of a specification (a written description of the invention), one or more claims, and drawings.

Your specification should present the most closely related prior art (previous contributions to the technology that your invention advances) of which you are aware. Intentionally omitting relevant information might result in the denial or invalidation of a patent.

Your specification also must include a description of what you believe to be the best mode for producing your invention. The language, here as elsewhere, must be straightforward and easily understood.

The claims section of your application requires particular care, because claims constitute the core of what you seek to protect. They are also the basis for court decisions regarding your patented invention.

Each claim is one sentence, usually consisting of a list of clauses. The claims section typically begins "I claim," "We claim," or "What is claimed is." The preamble, which is a summary of the type of invention you are seeking to patent (usually a brief phrase) comes next. In the transition, usually just the word "comprising," follows. Last is the body of the claim, listing the specific "elements"—the features of your invention, including those that are unique, that you want covered by the patent.

The Patent and Trademark Office also accepts claims in what is known as the Jepson-type format. This format contains a description of the invention's conventional or known elements in the claim's preamble, a transition phrase such as "wherein the improvement comprises," and the new or improved elements of the invention. Your patent attorney will know if the Jepson-type format is your best approach.

The patent attorney might want to use the means plus function format to claim your invention. This format expresses a means or step for performing a specified function without having to describe the structure, material, or acts required to perform that function. The means plus function format is helpful if describing the means by which your invention performs a function is easier than describing your invention's structure. Keep in mind, though, that courts generally limit the scope of any element described as a means plus function to devices or components which are actually described in the specification and equivalents thereof.

Another option is the product by process claim, in which you describe the process or method for producing your invention. This approach is sometimes problematic. In fact, until 1974, the Patent Office allowed product by process applications only when the invention was otherwise indescribable. The Patent Office's official policy has subsequently become somewhat more lenient.

A declaration, or oath, must accompany the patent application. Your signature on this document means that you reviewed and understood the patent application, that you believe you are the original inventor of what you seek to patent, and that you will give the Patent and Trademark Office any additional material it requests.

Fees. You also must enclose a fee with the patent application. The Patent and Trademark Office will levy additional fees based on the number and type of claims on your application. If your application is successful, the Patent Office will also charge you to issue the patent. You also must pay maintenance fees to keep an issued patent in force. These fees are listed in Appendix B.

Small entity status. You might be able to reduce many fees by 50 percent if you qualify for small entity status. To do this you must file a statement before or with the first fee you pay as a small entity, claiming that you are one of the following:

- a sole inventor who has not licensed or transferred the patent rights to anyone who is not a small entity

- one of two or more joint inventors, none of whom has licensed or otherwise transferred rights to the invention to anyone who is not a small entity

- a nonprofit organization

- a business with 500 or fewer full-time, part-time, and temporary employees during the business's fiscal year

Falsifying a small entity statement constitutes fraud and can result in rejection of the patent application or invalidation of an issued patent. An error not resulting from gross negligence can be corrected and excused during the pendency of the patent application by promptly notifying the Patent Office of the error and making up the difference in fees. However, because it is difficult to correct this error once the patent issues, it is advisable to redetermine your status each time a small entity fee is paid to the Patent Office.

Effective filing date for applications sent via Express Mail. The Patent and Trademark Office will accept your application's postmark as your filing date if you send the application via Express Mail. The application must bear a certificate of mailing by Express Mail signed by the person who mailed the package, and include the Express Mail label number, the date of mailing, and the title and address of the Commissioner of Patents and Trademarks. An example of a certificate of mailing by Express Mail can be found in Appendix G.

Using "Patent Pending." The period between the date your application is filed in the Patent and Trademark Office and the date the patent is granted or the application abandoned is the prosecution period. During this time, the application is said to be pending. While your application is pending, you can place the phrase "Patent Pending" or "Patent Applied For" on each copy of your invention, on products that embody your invention, and on literature and other materials relating to the invention. This notation signifies only that you have applied for a patent, not that the Patent and Trademark Office has begun to review the application or has granted a patent.

A "Patent Pending" notice gives you no legal protection. The notice might discourage competitors from copying your potentially patented invention, but it does not legally forbid them. Furthermore, a competitor may independently develop and market, without liability, a similar or identical invention during the period your patent is pending.

You should never mark products with a "Patent Pending" notice if you do not have a patent application on file with the U.S. Patent Office. Anyone can sue to stop such "false marking," and a fine of up to $500 for each product falsely marked can be assessed—half of which goes to the person bringing suit.

Information disclosure (or prior art) statement. Every individual associated with the filing of a patent application, including the inventor and the inventor's patent attorney, has a duty to disclose to the Patent Office information known to them that is material to the patentability of any claim in the application. Information is material if it is not cumulative to other information already of record and when it either:

- establishes, by itself or in combination with other information, a prima facie case of unpatentability; or

- refutes a position the applicant has taken in opposing a position taken by the Patent Office, or in asserting an argument of patentability.

A prima facie case of unpatentability occurs when every element of the claim in issue is found in a single prior art reference or in a combination of prior art references that include a suggestion to combine elements to produce the claimed invention. Failure to disclose known, material information in violation of the duty of disclosure can make your patent unenforceable against infringers.

The duty of disclosure is met by filing an information disclosure statement. An information disclosure statement includes a list of all patents, publications and other information submitted for consideration, a legible copy of the same, and a concise explanation of the relevance of each item submitted that is not in the English language. If a written English translation of a non-English language document, or a portion thereof, is in the possession or control of or is readily available to a person involved with the prosecution of the application, it must accompany the statement.

The information disclosure statement should be filed within three months of the U.S. filing date of the application, or before the mailing date of the first office action, whichever occurs last. An information disclosure statement that is filed after this period, but before the mailing date of a final action or a notice of allowance, will be considered by the Patent Office if it is accompanied by either:

(1) fee for late submission of an information disclosure statement (see Appendix B); or

(2) a certification that (a) each item of information contained in the information disclosure statement was cited in a communication from a foreign patent office in a counterpart foreign application not more than three months prior to the filing of the statement, or (b) that the information was not cited by a foreign patent office and was not known to any individual associated with the filing of the patent application more than three months prior to the filing of the statement. An information disclosure statement filed after a final action or a notice of allowance must be accompanied by the certification described above, a petition requesting consideration, and a petition fee (see Appendix B).

If you find you have not met the deadline for filing an information disclosure statement, you should consult with your attorney since it may be safer to file a continuation application than to file the required certification and/or a petition for the late information disclosure statement.

Application review. The Patent and Trademark Office will review your application for completeness shortly after receiving it. If the application is satisfactory, the office will assign it a filing date and a serial number, and will send it to the examination group assigned to your type of invention. The examination group, in turn, will send your application to one of its examiners. These first steps can take several months.

The examiner will review your application and, by means of an Office Action, will inform you that your application has been accepted and has proceeded to the next step, or that you need to make specified changes on the application to make it acceptable and what further information you should send. The examiner might issue several Office Actions, responding each time to your latest response.

Do not be discouraged if an examiner rejects many or even all of your original claims. He might simply want you to defend more extensively the claims you have made.

You are entitled to at least one further examination after receiving an Office Action. You can make none, some, or all of the examiner's suggested changes, additions, or deletions before requesting a further examination. Many applications generate several Office Actions and applicant responses before the Patent and Trademark Office approves further processing or issues a final rejection.

You normally need to respond to an Office Action within three months from the date the Patent and Trademark Office mailed it. The Patent and Trademark Office will grant an extension if you request it and include the required fee, but you cannot wait longer than six months to respond. If you do not file a response within six months (with the requisite fee for the extension period if your response is filed after three months), or if you fail to meet any other designated deadline, your application is abandoned, and you will not receive a patent.

Interviews. An examiner must grant an interview any time prior to a final office action. After a final office action, an examiner need not, but may, grant an interview. The interview may be with the inventor, the attorney, or both. An interview is particularly helpful if you do not understand the examiner's Office Actions, or if you wish to discuss possible amendments to the claims to overcome any prior art cited by the examiner. Interviews can be by telephone or in person at the U.S. Patent Office. The most effective interviews are in-person interviews, because they allow more dialogue between the examiner and the applicant or his representatives. However, this can be expensive if you live outside of the Arlington, VA/Washington, D.C. area.

Rejection. If the examiner concludes that you and he have insurmountable disagreements concerning one or more of your claims, he might issue a final rejection. You can cancel the disputed claims, change them to comply, file a continuation application to renew the entire process, or appeal the rejection to the Board of Appeals. If you are unsatisfied with the Board of Appeals' decision, you can appeal to the U.S. District Court in Washington, D.C., or to the U.S. Court of Appeals for the Federal Circuit.

Allowance. The correspondence between you and the examiner, if all goes well, will result in a Notice of Allowance, telling you that he considered the application to meet all the requirements for a patent. If you receive a Notice of Allowance, examine it carefully with your attorney. Check for a "reason for allowance" that your examiner might have listed. If a stated reason seems overly simple or inaccurate, notify the Patent Office; otherwise, you might encounter difficulties if your patent is later challenged.

Issuance. You have three months from the date the Patent Office mailed your Notice of Allowance to pay the issuance fee. Sometime thereafter, you should receive your Notice of Issuance, telling you your patent number and when the patent will be issued.

Errors and changes. When you get your patent, you and your attorney should check it for errors. To correct minor errors, such as typographical errors, file a petition for a certificate of correction. If the errors are the fault of the Patent and Trademark Office, there will be no fee. If the errors are your fault or your attorney's, you must enclose a fee. To correct more significant errors, you can apply for a patent reissue as long as the mistake was not intended to deceive anyone. You must surrender your original patent before you can get a reissued patent. Your reissued patent must not include anything new other than your corrections.

You also can try to change your patent in other ways. You can send the Patent and Trademark Office a statutory disclaimer, which retracts one or more of your patent claims. This is particularly important if you anticipate litigation concerning your patent and you believe your claims are too broad or otherwise invalid.

You also can narrow the scope of your patent claims by applying for a narrowing reissue. You may do this any time during the patent's term. This is usually more difficult than filing a statutory disclaimer, however. Your attorney will help you choose the best method for narrowing your claims.

On the other hand, you might wish to broaden your patent claims. You can do this by applying for a broadening reissue and filing the broadened claims within two years of the issuance date. You cannot, however, broaden your claims by filing for a corrective reissue.

Term of protection. A utility patent applied for after June 8, 1995, is valid for 20 years from the filing date of the application or, where the priority of an earlier application is claimed, from the filing date of the earliest application relied upon. Utility patents that were applied for, or were in force, prior to June 8, 1995, are valid for 17 years from date of issue or 20 years from the filing date, whichever is greater.

Maintenance fees. Maintenance fees must be paid on all U.S. utility patents filed after December 12, 1980, to keep the patents in force for the full term. Three maintenance fees are required. The first maintenance fee is due 3 1/2 years after a patent issues. A patent will expire on its fourth anniversary if the first maintenance fee is not paid. The second maintenance fee is due 7 1/2 years after a patent issues. A patent will expire on its eighth anniversary if the second maintenance fee is not paid. The third (and final) maintenance fee is due 11 1/2 years after a patent issues. A patent will expire on its twelfth anniversary if the third maintenance fee is not paid. (The current maintenance fees are shown in Appendix B.) If payment of a maintenance fee is accidentally and unintentionally missed, it may be possible to pay the maintenance fee late. In such cases, a penalty fee is always required, and a petition to revive the patent will be required if the mistake is not found until after the patent has expired for failure to pay the maintenance fee. A patent that has expired for failure to pay a maintenance fee cannot be revived if the mistake is discovered more than 24 months after the patent expired.

Patent marks. You should notify people who see or use your invention that it is protected. The best way is to place the word "Patent," or the abbreviation "Pat.," and the number of your patent on each copy of your invention, and also on the patented part of any product that embodies your invention. This notice is not mandatory, but it is advisable. It discourages would-be infringers, and enables you to recover damages for infringement that occurs before the filing of a patent infringement lawsuit.

Do not place a patent notice on anything not yet patented. Nor should you mark anything "Patent Pending" unless you really have applied for a patent. Intentional false marking is a criminal offense. As noted previously, you can be fined up to $500 for each offense.

Your rights. As a patent owner, you have exclusive rights in your invention. A patent does not give you permission to practice or use your invention, although you do have that right, as long as doing so does not infringe someone else's patent. Instead, a patent gives you the right to exclude others from making, using, offering for sale, or selling the invention for as long as your patent remains in effect. In this regard, a patent is a "negative right."

A patent is personal property. Accordingly, you can grant others permission to use, promote, or sell your patented invention. Typically, a license is granted to another party in exchange for a royalty or other form of compensation. If you grant an exclusive license, you cannot later license someone else to use your invention. Your compensation, therefore, usually will be higher than for nonexclusive licenses. You would be well-advised to have an attorney draft your licensing contracts.

Foreign patent protection. Patent protection in foreign countries usually will cost you more than protection in the U.S. As with copyright protection, there is no "international patent" that protects your invention everywhere. In many cases, the trouble and expense of foreign protection is unjustifiable.

Some countries charge high filing fees. Most charge annual maintenance fees that increase each year. Gaining foreign protection often requires hiring a lawyer or agent in each country. If you file your foreign applications within one year of your U.S. filing date, you can get the benefit of your U.S. filing date in many countries. If you wish to obtain foreign patents in countries that are members of one or more international patent treaties, you must file corresponding foreign applications within one year of your U.S. filing date if you have begun commercial use, or have published your invention after your U.S. filing date and before your foreign filing date.

Because filing patent applications in each country can be expensive, you might be better off relying on an international patent treaty. Not all countries are parties to a treaty, but many countries are. This route usually is less expensive than country-by-country filing if protection is sought in five or so member countries.

One such treaty to which the United States belongs is the Patent Cooperation Treaty (PCT). A PCT application can be filed by transmitting to the U.S. Receiving Office for the PCT (located in the U.S. Patent Office) a copy of the U.S. application, the formal application documents which designate the member countries[9] in which the application is to be filed, and the fee. A PCT application must be filed within one year of the filing date of a U.S. patent application, and is typically filed to extend the time for foreign filing while preserving your foreign filing rights. Once the PCT application is filed, the applicant will have to enter the National Phase in each desired country. In order to enter the National Phase, local counsel must be selected, a filing fee must be paid, and translations may be required for each non-English speaking PCT country where a patent is desired. The National Phase must be entered within 20 months after the U.S. filing date unless a preliminary examination is requested, in which case the National Phase must be entered within 30 months after the U.S. filing date. Discuss this option with your attorney if you seek protection in several countries who are members of the PCT.

The European Patent Convention (EPC) can give you protection in most Western European countries.[10] To obtain EPC protection, you can submit a PCT application through the U.S. Receiving Office (by listing the EPC as a selected country), or through an attorney or agent in one of the EPC countries. Your application will be examined by the European Patent Office (EPO) in Munich, West Germany. If your application succeeds, the EPO will send copies to each designated member country. On payment of a fee and filing of a translation, each country then issues

---

[9]A list of the PCT member countries as of May 1999 can be found in Appendix H.

[10]EPC members are listed in Appendix H.

---

you its own patent, which will be valid for 20 years from your EPC filing date if the annual maintenance fees are paid.

If someone infringes your patent. Patent litigation is almost always more complicated than litigation concerning other forms of intellectual property. Patent litigation might include suing someone for infringement, or being sued by someone who wants to invalidate your patent. It is usually better to settle out of court, unless the potential market for the disputed item is very large. Patent-related suits typically cost more than $500,000 to take to trial. Since this is beyond the means of many individuals and small business owners, you may wish to seek patent enforcement insurance for your most valuable patents.

You cannot sue someone for patent infringement until the Patent and Trademark Office has issued the patent. Thereafter, you can sue or seek other means to recover damages, or both.

For instance, you can sue someone who is producing or marketing your patented invention without your permission. You would sue him for direct infringement of your patent.

You can sue someone who knowingly encourages or helps another person infringe your patent. You would sue him for inducement of infringement.

Contributory infringers constitute another category of individuals you can sue. A contributory infringer is someone who sells items that can only be used to infringe your patent, sold knowingly in violation of your patent.

If you are accused of infringement. An accusation of infringement can be as plain as a lawsuit, or as innocent as a letter advising you of the existence of a patent and inviting you to consider taking a license. Both should be treated seriously to avoid any claim that the alleged infringement is willful. An infringement is willful if the accused infringer does not act as a reasonable, prudent person would have acted when faced with the claim of infringement. If willful infringement is found by a court, triple damages can be assessed and the infringer can be required to pay the patentee's attorneys' fees and court costs (which can range from several hundred thousand dollars to millions of dollars). Because such damages and costs can reach a level that is beyond the means of all but the largest of companies, a competent patent attorney should be consulted promptly when a claim of infringement is received.

The first thing the patent attorney will do is examine the patent and its Patent Office file to determine the scope of the patent claims. To determine infringement, the accused infringing device or method will be compared to the claims of the patent. If each and every element found in the claims is also found in the device or method alleged to be an infringement, then the device or method technically infringes the patent. To avoid a finding of willfulness, and to avoid the assessment of further damages, the device or method should be modified so that it does not fall within the scope of the claims. You may be able to do this, for example, by a redesign that eliminates from the device or method one or more of the elements of the claim. Your patent attorney should be able to assist you in determining whether your redesign is sufficient to avoid infringement.

If you cannot redesign your device or method, you may be able to defend yourself by showing that the patent is invalid. This is very difficult to do, however, because the level of evidence required to prove invalidity—"clear and convincing"—is very high.

To succeed in proving that the patent is invalid, you must present clear and convincing evidence that the invention is not novel, is obvious, is not useful, or is insufficiently disclosed in the patent specification. This can be done, for example, by using publications that were published more than a year before the filing date of the patent and that show the claimed invention or an obvious variation. This can also be done by showing that the patented invention itself was sold or offered for sale more than a year before the filing date of the patent. The court will assume that the patent is valid because the Patent and Trademark Office issued it, and you must present clear evidence that was not before the Patent Office to overcome this assumption.

Another possible defense is to establish that the patent holder was dishonest in his dealings with the Patent and Trademark Office. This entails proving intentional misrepresentation. If you prove this, the court might rule that the patent is unenforceable and that you are not liable to the plaintiff. The court also might impose punishment on the plaintiff. Keep in mind that this defense is also difficult to prove, since it requires clear and convincing evidence. This burden is further complicated by the difficulties in obtaining evidence establishing the patentee's intent to mislead the patent office.

If the patentee actually knew, or should have known, about the accused infringing activity and held off filing a lawsuit for a long time, the accused infringer may be able to avoid pre-lawsuit damages by asserting the defense of laches. This defense has a lower burden of proof (preponderance of the evidence) and is frequently granted where the patentee has delayed filing suit for more than 6 years. In the unusual case where the patentee has implicitly or expressly communicated an intent not to enforce, and the accused infringer acted in reliance on the patentee's misleading action (e.g., by expanding its business or market), the accused infringer may be able to assert the defense of estoppel. If the Court finds that estoppel applies, the patent will likely not be enforceable at all against the accused infringer. There are other defenses that can be raised, depending on the factual circumstances of the case. Your patent attorney should be able to determine which defenses should be raised in the event of a patent infringement lawsuit.

You also can seek to prove that the patent owner misused his patent, e.g., by violating antitrust laws. The court might excuse you from damages the plaintiff incurred while he was misusing his patent. You cannot use this defense if the patent owner was using the patent in a way that would constitute infringement if anyone else used it, if he permitted someone else to use the patent in that way, or if he tried to enforce his patent against infringement.

If a patent owner accuses you of infringing a patent, and he threatens to sue you but has not yet filed against you, you can initiate a lawsuit against him to declare the patent invalid and/or not infringed. Making the first move gives you the advantage, because you, the plaintiff, have more control over where the case will be heard. Being the plaintiff also gives you the advantage if you agree to settle out of court.

Computer software. For many years, the U.S. Patent Office took the position that computer software could not be patented. As a result of several important legal decisions, the Patent Office has changed its position and will allow certain kinds of software patents. While a mathematical algorithm, or software that merely implements a mathematical algorithm, cannot be patented, software using algorithms to achieve a useful result (e.g., transformation of data for use in a process or for use to create a product) can be patented. As before, the process followed by the software in achieving the useful result can also be claimed as a process. Claiming the process in conjunction with a computer can often prevent competitors from practicing the most useful implementation of the idea. This area of the law is in its infancy and is expected to rapidly evolve. Accordingly, any inventor wishing to obtain patent protection for software should seek assistance from an experienced patent attorney.

DESIGN PATENTS

Design patents protect an original appearance given to an object. These patents cover only novel and nonobvious appearances. Design patents, unlike utility patents, are issued only to ornamental, nonfunctional aspects of a manufactured item. Rather than protecting an item, a design patent protects only an item's appearance. Design patents generally are cheaper and faster to obtain than utility patents.

The application. A design patent application requires particularly detailed drawings. You must include several views of the design so that the appearance of the design cannot be mistaken.

The specification of a design patent application needs to include explanations only of the drawings. The claims section should have only one claim, which indicates the nature or type of manufactured item on which the design is to appear.

In most other respects, applying for a design patent is similar to applying for a utility patent. You might require the services of an attorney.

Term of protection. A design patent is valid for a period of 14 years. No maintenance fees are required to keep design patents in effect for their full term.

Infringement. Infringement of a design patent is handled similarly to infringement of a utility patent. You will need an attorney to handle your case.

TRADE SECRETS

Trade secrets are more difficult to protect than other kinds of intellectual property. This is principally because trade secret law is the subject of state, rather than federal, law. Many states, including California, have enacted the Uniform Trade Secrets Act, or amended versions thereof, along with criminal laws punishing the theft of trade secrets. In addition, there is a substantial body of common law[11] dealing with trade secrets. Although trade secret laws can vary widely between states, such laws can be quite protective if the proper precautionary steps are taken.

WHAT IS A TRADE SECRET?

A trade secret can be any information that derives actual or potential economic value from not being generally known to others and that is the subject of reasonable efforts to maintain its secrecy. Secret or confidential information that gives your business an advantage over competitors who do not have the same information can be a trade secret. Trade secrets might include a chemical formula, a manufacturing process, a technique, a design, computer software, an advertising strategy, a customer list, or a company budget. Because trade secret law is not governed by statute, the range of protectable information is virtually unlimited.

There are two reasons you should be aware of trade secret law. If you own a business, you probably want to protect your company secrets. Conversely, if you are employed by a company, but are planning to start your own business in competition with your current employer, you will not want your employer to sue you for stealing his trade secrets.

---

[11] Common law comes from the rulings of judges in lawsuits.

HOW TO PROTECT YOUR TRADE SECRETS

In most cases, you should be able to design your own trade secret protection system. You probably will not need a lawyer to help you, unless you plan to use special legal contracts and agreements.

Identifying your trade secrets. The first step in protecting your trade secrets is to identify them. For example, you might consider the following items to be valuable trade secrets.

- employee salaries
- customer lists
- sources and suppliers
- the process for manufacturing your product
- computer program source codes
- advertising methods and plans.
- plans for future products
- in-house procedure or policy manuals
- manufacturing costs
- sales and profit figures

In short, you should identify everything you do not want your competitors to know. Trade secrets cannot, however, include general business practices, such as how often you update ledgers or how your employees answer the telephone. Trade secrets, by definition, do not include anything about your company, its products, or its practices that is publicly known.

Controlling access. Restrict access to sensitive trade secrets as much as possible, and keep records of who has access to which secrets. This practice will help you limit and trace leaks. More importantly, it will show that you considered the information to be a trade secret. Also, to the extent that you can, keep sensitive information away from photocopying machines and other means of copying or disseminating material.

Nondisclosure agreements. You should consider requiring your employees to sign a nondisclosure agreement. This is a document stating that the employee agrees to keep confidential, during and following his employment, information about the company that, if revealed outside the company, will be detrimental. Keep the terms broad enough to cover potential changes in what you consider a trade secret, but not so broad as to render the document unclear or unenforceable. To be enforceable, some "consideration" must be given for the employee's promise. For new employees, the employment itself is sufficient. For current employees, continuing employment is not sufficient: a small sum of money, a promotion, bonus, or advantageous change in benefits can be sufficient consideration for signing the agreement.

Often, the principal value of a nondisclosure agreement is as a deterrent, because a court will not always consider such an agreement fully binding on an employee. If a nondisclosure agreement becomes relevant in a lawsuit involving trade secrets, the court will judge the extent of the document's enforceability according to certain criteria, for example, whether or not the information was really secret, whether or not the source of the information was marked as confidential, and so forth.

An explicit nondisclosure agreement might not be necessary. A court might recognize a confidentiality pledge implicit in the nature of an employee's work. This depends on how confidential the information handled by the employee was, how valuable to the company the information was, how closely guarded the information was, and other factors.

Keeping records. Be ready to document dollar amounts, in case the value of certain information is debated. Keep logs that detail research and development expenditures, and maintain ledgers that demonstrate revenues earned expressly from your trade secrets. Good records can help enormously in court.

Noncompetition agreements. Noncompetition agreements are also advisable.[12] An employee signing one agrees not to enter business in direct competition with your company. You must be careful with these agreements, however, and you should consult an attorney before drafting and implementing them. They must not unreasonably restrict an employee from earning a living if he leaves your company. In some states, noncompetition agreements might not be entirely enforceable. Statutes do not grant validity to such agreements in those states except in some very limited circumstances.

A departing employee. An employee who leaves your company to work for a competitor will probably know some of your trade secrets. In most cases, you cannot stop him from joining a competitor, but you can minimize the risk of the employee accidentally or intentionally revealing those secrets to his new employer. You might, for example, tell your departing employee, in writing and in

---

[12]A typical noncompetition agreement appears in Appendix F.

an exit interview, what you consider a trade secret and that, even though he is leaving your employ, he is still obligated to maintain confidentiality. You cannot, however, prevent him from disclosing some of your company's general business practices or other general information.

Naturally, it is preferable to avoid litigation. Doing your best to prevent trade secret disclosure is far better than pursuing through the courts someone who has already revealed your valuable secrets.

HOW TO AVOID STEALING TRADE SECRETS

By the same token, you as an employer can take steps to avoid unethical or illegal procurement of a competitor's trade secrets. Proper action now might keep you out of court and will protect your professional reputation.

Hiring away from a competitor. If you hire someone who has worked for a competitor, be sure the new employee understands that he is not to reveal his former company's trade secrets. You also might send the former employer a polite letter that states you have prohibited the new employee from giving you confidential information about that company. Such a letter will indicate that you are conscientious and ethical and might prevent frivolous suits in the future.

Accidental access to trade secrets. If, despite your precautions, you accidentally receive a competitor's trade secret, keep track of where and how you obtained it. If the information becomes well known, it will lose its trade secret status and its legal protection.

COMPETING WITH A FORMER EMPLOYER

You must be particularly careful if you leave your employer and establish your own business in competition with him. (This is especially true if you have signed a noncompetition agreement.) The former employer is bound to feel vulnerable toward an ex-employee who knows a number of trade secrets. This feeling might lead to legal action, merited or not.

Hiring former coworkers. The more employees you hire away from your former employer, the more worried he is likely to be. Taking coworkers with you when you start your own business requires careful maneuvering. Courts have levied sizeable damages against former employees who have recruited unethically. It is advisable to consult an attorney before you ask coworkers to quit with you to join your new company. Usually, you will be safer if you refrain from recruiting until your resignation is effective. In fact, you are safest if you refrain from even discussing your plans to form a competing company until you have left your employer.

Customer lists. Avoid taking or using customer lists that belong to your former employer, even if you compiled the lists yourself. They belong to him, and he might sue you if you use them. The more carefully your former employer guarded his customer lists, the more legally liable you are held for using them. Customer lists are often considered one of the most valuable kinds of trade secrets.

Corporate opportunity laws. Some states require you to present potential money-making ideas to your employer before you quit to form your own company with the idea. Consult a lawyer to see if your idea falls under corporate opportunity laws, if your state has them.

SUING TRADE SECRET "THIEVES"

Lawsuits associated with trade secrets are costly for both the plaintiff and defendant in time, emotional energy, and money. As with all kinds of intellectual property, both sides usually win something when they settle out of court, and both lose to varying degrees when they take their differences to a judge. This is especially true in trade secret cases because of the tremendous amount of money required for court resolution.

It is, unfortunately, sometimes impossible to settle out of court. Although you probably should hire a lawyer if you intend to settle out of court, you will certainly need one to represent you if you go to court, either as plaintiff or defendant.

Whom you can sue. You may take legal action against the person or persons who had original access to your trade secrets, and against the individuals and companies who obtain the secrets from the "thieves." Nevertheless, you probably never will recover everything you have lost, even if you win a lawsuit.

Temporary restraining order. If a judge will not immediately issue an injunction, he might issue a *temporary restraining order*, which will put the case on hold until an injunction hearing takes place. Temporary restraining orders are less restrictive than injunctions, however, and usually remain valid for a shorter period (20 days).

Preliminary injunction. You probably will want to obtain a preliminary injunction. This is a court order forbidding the defendant from using what you claim to be your trade secret until after a full trial is concluded. A judge might decide to issue an injunction immediately, or he might decide to hold an injunction hearing, during which both sides present testimony to prove whether or not an injunction is warranted.

It might take you about 30 days to obtain a preliminary injunction once you have filed a motion with the court. If the judge grants your motion for a summary judgment, you will usually be required to post a reasonable bond sufficient to cover any damages suffered by the enjoined party as a result of the preliminary injunction if you lose the lawsuit. If an injunction is issued, and the defendant violates it, he could be cited for contempt of court. An injunction could greatly hinder the defendant's business, but a failure to obtain an injunction could result in disclosure and destruction of your trade secrets while the lawsuit is pending.

Discovery. Prior to trial, both sides will engage in a period of discovery, during which each side collects from the other documents that could be relevant to the case. The discovery might also include depositions of employees in both companies and of third parties, such as vendors and customers. This takes a great deal of time and adds considerably to the growing expense of the lawsuit.

Expert witnesses. You might need to hire experts from outside your company to testify on your behalf. For instance, an economist who specializes in your field might be able to estimate your losses resulting from the alleged trade secret theft. An independent source usually is perceived by judges and juries as more legitimate; however, an expert witness's testimony will cost you money.

The trial date. The preliminary preparation for trial will almost certainly take several months and may take more than a year. When a trial date finally is set, your attorney will need to devote a larger proportion of his time to your case, because he will be working with a deadline. Your attorney probably charges you by the hour, so this period and the trial itself will result in your greatest expenses.[13] Nothing—other than pride, perhaps—prevents you from settling with the defendant at this juncture. Many trade secret cases end in an out-of-court settlement, saving both sides the effort, legal fees, and invaluable time consumed by a trial.

---

[13] You might instead hire your lawyer on a contingency basis, whereby he is paid a predetermined amount or percentage of damages only if you win the case. This fee basis, however, is rare in trade secret cases. More common is the value-determined basis, which entails set fees for the entire case, regardless of the outcome or the number of hours it takes.

IF YOU ARE SUED

If you are a defendant in a lawsuit over trade secrets, you should consider, with your counsel, several strategies and tactics. The best defenses require action before a lawsuit ensues.

Keeping records. Accurate, detailed records that document how you developed your own customer lists and your own products, and how you obtained your employees, will prove invaluable if you are sued for stealing trade secrets or for unfairly recruiting employees from another company. During the discovery stage of trade secret proceedings, your opponent has access to every interview, conversation, letter, and document to which you were a party, except communications with your lawyer and, sometimes, with your spouse. It pays to keep copies of the polite letters you have written to your new employee's former boss, and to emphasize to third parties that you bear no malice toward your former employer. Such evidence, when produced in court, might help convince a judge that you are not the "thief" the plaintiff claims you are.

Counter-complaints. Your attorney might advise you to proceed aggressively. If the plaintiff's case is weak, one tactic is to file a counter-complaint against the plaintiff, claiming he is guilty of holding invalid patents or violating antitrust laws, for example. This counterattack might help persuade the plaintiff to settle with you out of court.

TRADEMARKS

A trademark is a word, name, or symbol that you use to distinguish your products or services from those of your competitors. It usually is a brand name or logo that appears on your products. Trademarks are valuable to you because they let your customers know which goods or services are yours, and that you assure the consistent quality of those goods or services. This section also covers other, related marks.

CATEGORIES OF MARKS

Marks fall into four categories. One is trademarks. Service marks are those marks you use in selling or advertising your services to distinguish them from your competitors' services. Certification marks are those marks you use on products or in connection with services provided by someone other than the mark's owner, which certify their quality, accuracy, origin, material, manufacturing method, or other characteristics. Collective marks are those marks you use to indicate that you are a member of a cooperative, association, or other collective organization. You can register as collective membership marks those marks that indicate your membership in a union, association, or other organization.

CHOOSING TRADEMARKS

Select your trademarks with care. The way your chosen trademarks relate to your products determines the degree to which they are protected.

Coined marks. The greatest protection is given to a trademark that you coin and that bears not even the slightest suggestion of the nature of your product (e.g., the name "Kodak" on cameras). A coined mark is favored in court because it is intrinsically distinctive, and therefore it is unlikely to be already in use on other products. Thus, it is rarely difficult to register a coined mark, and it can be used on a variety of products you might produce.

Arbitrary marks. The next best choice is a mark that consists of a word already in existence, but arbitrary as applied to your product (e.g., the name "Crest" on toothpaste). You can register an arbitrary mark if its use would not confuse consumers, but you probably will have to limit its use to a particular product or narrow range of products.

Suggestive marks. A suggestive mark, which hints at the nature of the product under that mark, is entitled to less protection than a coined or arbitrary mark. An example of a suggestive mark is the name "Black Flag" on a household pesticide. You might encounter some difficulty registering a suggestive mark, depending on the degree to which it suggests the nature or attributes of your product.

Descriptive marks. Descriptive marks are very difficult to register and protect. In fact, a descriptive mark (e.g., the name "Cat Chow" on cat food) normally cannot be registered until, after a period of heavy use, the mark becomes associated virtually exclusively with your product. It takes a significant amount of consumer identification for a descriptive mark to be considered registrable.

Generic marks. Generic names (e.g., the words "Beer" or "Aspirin") cannot be protected as trademarks. Such names do not distinguish one company's product from its competitors'.

What cannot be registered as a trademark. You cannot register a trademark that is immoral, deceptive, or scandalous; that defames an institution, belief, national symbol, or a living or deceased person; or that contains the flag or other insignia of a country, state, or municipality. Also, you cannot use the name, portrait, or signature of a living person unless you have his written permission, and you cannot use the name, portrait, or signature of a deceased U.S. president during his widow's life without her written permission.

Avoiding trademark loss. Trademarks can lose protection by becoming generic names. "Aspirin" was originally a trademark that became a generic descriptive term for acetylsalicylic acid because people used it to describe the product rather than the brand name. Other examples are "Band-Aid," as applied to an adhesive bandage strip, and "Kleenex," as applied to a facial tissue.

You might avoid losing your trademark protection in this manner by always referring to your product by the trademark plus the generic type of product (e.g., "Kleenex brand facial tissues"), rather than using the trademark alone to denote the product. Some companies spend many advertising dollars reminding the public not to use their trademark as a generic term. If you fear your trademark is becoming generic, you might want to do the same.

You also can lose trademark protection by abandoning your mark. Trademark protection ordinarily lasts as long as you continually use the mark, if you renew it every 10 years. If you stop using the mark for a significant period of time, you might lose your rights in that mark. If you do not use it for a two-year period, the mark is presumed to be abandoned. An abandoned mark is available to anyone who wishes to use it, and can be registered by another party that has adopted it.

State protection. Trademarks can be protected in your state, if you do not desire federal protection or such protection is unavailable to you. A trademark attorney in your state will be able to help you. State registration alone might be significantly less protective, however.

HOW TO REGISTER YOUR MARKS

You can register your trademarks with the U.S. Patent and Trademark Office. You must use the trademark with goods or services in interstate commerce in order to obtain a federal trademark registration. However, you may file an Intent-To-Use application prior to actual use if you wish to reserve a trademark. An individual, firm, partnership, corporation, or association can own and register a trademark.

You must own a mark to register it. When requesting the proper forms from the Patent and Trademark Office, specify whether you are applying as an individual, a firm, or a corporation.

Trademark search. You should have an attorney conduct a trademark search before you begin to use and register your mark. You can file a trademark registration application yourself, but you might want an attorney to handle it because registration requirements are very strict.

The application and drawing. You need to submit a written application; a drawing of the mark; for a conventional application, identical specimens or facsimiles; and a fee. No specimens are required for an Intent-To-Use application. The application is fairly straightforward. Specifications for the drawing, however, are numerous and detailed. For a word mark, block letters must be used. For a logo or design mark, the drawing must exactly represent your mark, must be in pure black India ink on standard-size white paper, must contain no white correction fluid, and must have a heading that includes your name, address, the date of the mark's first use, and the goods or services listed in the application. Send the drawing flat, with adequate protection, or rolled in a mailing tube.

The specimens or facsimiles. The specimens you submit must have the trademark somewhere on the product itself or on a label, tag, container, or display associated with or attached to the product. You normally cannot use advertising materials as specimens. The specimens must be flat and no larger than 8 1/2 × 13 inches. For service marks, company business cards, brochures, or photographs of signage bearing the mark may serve as specimens.

If your specimens are too bulky or are not flat, you may instead submit facsimiles of the trademark as it is used. Facsimiles may be photographs or other clear reproductions, no larger than 8 1/2 × 13 inches.

The Patent and Trademark Office is more lenient in its requirements for service mark specimens or facsimiles. If you cannot submit specimens or facsimiles due to the way the mark is used, you may submit a letter of explanation.

The fee. You must include a filing fee with your application. Fees current as of the date of printing of this book are found in Appendix B. These fees should be checked for accuracy by contacting the Trademark Office using the contact information contained in Appendix A. Your payment must be payable to the Commissioner of Patents and Trademarks.

The application review. The Patent and Trademark Office reviews trademark applications in the order in which they are received. If, after a preliminary study of your application, an examiner requests more information from you, you must respond within six months or the office will consider your application abandoned.

Rejection and appeal. If the application is rejected, the office will notify you and give you its reasons. You can appeal to the Trademark Trial and Appeal Board, if you wish. There is an appeal fee.

Publication for Opposition. If no reason is found to deny registration of your trademark, the examiner will send the application to the publications branch, where your trademark will be published for opposition in the *Trademark Official Gazette*. Anyone who might be damaged by the registration of your trademark will then have 30 days from the date of publication to oppose the registration or to file an extension of time to oppose. If no oppositions or requests for extension of time to oppose are received by the Trademark Office during the 30-day period, the application will be approved and the trademark will be registered, unless the application was an ITU application. ITU applications are registered only after use of the trademark in interstate commerce begins and a timely statement of use is filed.

The registers. A successful application will allow your mark to be listed on one of two trademark registers. Coined, arbitrary, and suggestive marks, if qualified, will be registered on the Principal Register. This is the best register on which to list your mark, because inclusion on this register constitutes constructive notice of your rights in that mark. Your rights in the mark are difficult to challenge because marks on the Principal Register carry a presumption of validity. After five years on the Principal Register, you can file an affidavit of continuing use under Section 8 and Section 15 of the Trademark Act and your registration will become incontestable. This means a challenger cannot cancel your registration without proof of fraud committed in order to obtain the registration.

Marks that do not qualify for the Principal Register but have been used commercially for at least a year and serve to distinguish your products or services from those of someone else will be added to the Supplemental Register. Although a mark on the Supplemental Register does not carry the same strong presumptions as one on the Principal Register, you may ask a court to help preserve your rights in the mark if you feel the mark is being infringed. A mark on the Supplemental Register can be transferred later to the Principal Register if the mark becomes eligible.

Continued use. To keep your registration in force, you need to file with the Patent and Trademark Office, between the fifth and sixth year following the original registration's issue date, an affidavit of continued use. You might have to send proof that you are still using the mark. Such proof might include product packaging or advertising that bears both the mark and an indication of the product or service attributes your customers associate with the mark.

Renewal. Trademark registrations issued before November 16, 1989 expire 20 years after the registration issues. Registrations issued on or after November 16, 1989 expire 10 years after the registration issues. You can renew either type of registration for further 10-year periods by filing a renewal application during the six-month period prior to the expiration date. Such applications may also be filed during the three-month period after the expiration date if an additional fee is paid. Renewal applications are handled much like initial applications, and require a specimen of the mark, a renewal fee, and a statement that the mark is still in use.

TRADEMARK NOTICE

As with copyrights and patents, trademarks require that you give adequate public notice that your mark is protected in order to achieve maximum protection against infringers. The symbol TM, often used as a superscript, indicates that the word or design preceding it is claimed as a trademark by the owner. Once federal registration is obtained for the mark, always place with the mark the words "Registered in U.S. Patent and Trademark Office," the abbreviations "Reg. U.S. Pat. and Tm. Off." or the symbol ® (the letter R in a circle) to denote the registered trademark. This is used instead of the symbol TM. You cannot use "®", "Reg. U.S. Pat and Tm. Off." or "Registered in U.S. Patent and Trademark Office" if your mark is registered only in your state or if you claim only common law trademark rights.

FOREIGN TRADEMARK PROTECTION

Foreign trademark protection is relatively easy to obtain, frequently even before you begin to use the mark in the desired countries. Unlike in the United States, the right to use trademarks in most countries comes from a trademark registration and not from use. For this reason, you should think about registering your key trademarks worldwide, or at least in countries where you are likely to do business in the future. A company failing to follow this precaution may have to pay significant sums for a foreign "entrepreneur" who registers in his own country a key trademark belonging to the U.S. company and subsequently uses the registration to prevent the company from selling products in that country under the trademark.

PROTECTING YOUR TRADEMARK

You have the right to use your trademark to distinguish your products or services from your competitors'. If a competitor uses your mark, or one similar enough when applied to goods or services to confuse a consumer, you must take steps to protect your mark and the goodwill it represents.

Infringement. You have legal recourse if you believe someone is infringing your trademark, even if the alleged infringement is unintentional. The first step, of course, is to hire an attorney.

You might be able to obtain an injunction against someone whom you can prove is about to infringe your trademark. This would prevent possible infringement until a trial can determine conclusively whether or not the new mark infringes yours.

You also can ask a judge to issue a writ of attachment if you believe the defendant might move his funds abroad to prevent losing them to you in court. A writ of attachment prevents the defendant from moving his funds until the trial ends.

After an infringement occurs, you can sue for damages as well as for an injunction. A judge might award you part or all of the infringer's profits or your lost profits. If the infringer's actions have been blatantly illegal, the judge might grant you punitive damages and attorneys' fees, as well. He also might award you a combination of these damages. The judge can also enter an injunction that prohibits the sale of goods with the infringing mark. If the mark cannot be obliterated, removed, or destroyed without destroying the goods, the judge may order the goods be turned over to you.

TRADE NAMES AND FICTITIOUS NAMES

A trade name is simply the name by which the public knows your business. It is virtually the same as a fictitious name, which is a commercially used name that does not fully identify its user.

REGISTRATION

Both trade names and fictitious names can be registered with most state governments. If your trade name is also a fictitious name, you probably can protect it by registering it as one or the other. Trade name registration is usually stronger. Contact the appropriate government office in your state.

INTELLECTUAL PROPERTY AND THE INTERNET

The explosive growth of the internet has created unprecedented opportunities for entrepreneurs. It has also created a legal minefield for the unwary that affects every kind of intellectual property.

The principal difficulty is that intellectual property laws are inherently national in character, and typically stop at the border. The internet, on the other hand, is a vast, new, worldwide marketplace that cuts across national borders. Internet advertising offers significantly greater impact than conventional, local advertising—a potential audience many magnitudes larger combined with exposure of a greater duration at much less expense. More important, the internet offers interactive communication between buyers and sellers in different states or countries. This fact creates enforcement problems for the owners of intellectual property. It also exposes unwary sellers to potentially devastating legal problems.

PATENTS

For owners of U.S. patents, the internet represents a new marketplace that should be monitored for enforcement purposes. Patents can only be enforced within the countries that issue them. Suppose you own a U.S. patent, but no related foreign patents. A manufacturer in Germany could make, use, or sell your patented invention anywhere in the world, except the United States, without liability. But suppose the German manufacturer used the internet to advertise the sale of your invention to customers everywhere in the world. Offering a patented invention for sale without the authorization of the patent owner is an act of infringement in the United States. But where would you file the infringement lawsuit if letters fail to stop the offending internet advertisements? Would you have to travel to Germany? Probably not. At present, you can probably file such a lawsuit in the United States. However, if the German manufacturer is small and does not have property (or a presence) in the United States, it might successfully challenge personal jurisdiction, or simply refuse to come to the United States to defend the lawsuit. In either event, satisfying a judgment or enforcing an injunction against such a company would be problematic.

In addition, vigilance is needed because such internet advertisements may start the clock running on defenses like laches, even if you don't know that the advertisements are there. Because the internet is publicly available, and readily searchable, courts may, in the future, rule on laches defenses in favor of accused infringers on the basis that the patent owner "should have known" of the accused infringing activity based on the accused infringer's internet advertising. Accordingly, you should monitor the internet on a regular basis (including competitors' websites) to locate potential infringements, and keep records that establish your methodology and diligence. That way, if laches is asserted against you in the future you will be able to persuade the court that you did not know of the accused infringing activity even though you acted in a reasonable and prudent manner under the circumstances to search out such activity.

TRADEMARKS AND TRADE NAMES

Trademark owners have discovered several significant enforcement problems arising from the use of the internet. One problem arises from the use and adoption of a trademark owned by another. For example, suppose a merchant in Georgia adopts and uses on the internet the mark "Zapper" for a radar countermeasure device. You own a registration in California for "Zapper" for identical goods. While you certainly have the right to enforce your trademark in California (and may lose your rights to the trademark if you don't), you may or may not be able to sue the Georgia merchant in California. A similar problem can arise between the owner of a U.S. registered trademark and the owner of a foreign registered trademark. This situation should be promptly brought to the attention of your intellectual property attorney, as the laws in this area are changing rapidly.

Another problem occurs when someone registers a domain name that is identical to another company name or registered trademark. Many large, well-known U.S. organizations have discovered this problem when they attempt to register a domain name and are refused because there is a prior registrant. Frequently, the prior registrant is a domain name pirate who registers the domain name only so that he can offer to sell the domain name to the organization for a large sum of money. The potential for this misuse is significant, particularly for organizations with many well-known trademarks. For example, if a domain name pirate chooses to prey on Coca Cola, Inc., he might seek to register the following domain names.

Coca-cola.com	Cocacola.com	Cocacolas.com
Cocacola.org	Coke.com	Cokes.com
Coke.org	Sprite.com	etc.

At present, the owners of registered trademarks can have such domain names placed on hold by following the procedure established by the organization responsible for assigning domain names. Such procedures frequently change, increasing the difficulty of enforcement. Of course, owners of federal registrations for famous marks can also sue domain name pirates. While simply registering a trademark as a domain name, without more, is not commercial use of a trademark (and therefore not trademark infringement), such activity does constitute trademark dilution under both federal and state laws.

To avoid these problems, trademark owners should register and engage in at least minimal use of domain names that correspond to their company name and most important trademarks.

TRADE SECRETS

The ease of uploading information onto the internet for broad-based distribution increases the difficulty of safeguarding trade secrets. The threat is both external and internal. The problem of hackers gaining access to a computer system has been a problem for many years, and the internet may provide new portals of entry for hackers. In addition, disaffected employees or ex-employees can more easily destroy critical trade secrets stored on a computer by simply uploading them to the internet. To avoid these kinds of problems, you may wish to consult with computer experts and implement appropriate safety precautions to limit access to your most important trade secrets and prevent transfer and/or copying of that information.

COPYRIGHTS

The reproduction of copyrighted materials on the internet is a massive problem. Virtually any two-dimensional copyrighted material can be posted anonymously and downloaded and reproduced by anyone having access to the internet. For example, photographs appearing in adult content magazines are frequently posted on the internet, and then reproduced on multiple sites on the internet, creating an enforcement nightmare for the copyright owner. Problems can arise for organizations that reproduce and/or assist in the transmission of such material. Certainly, website operators and others who charge a subscription fee or a set charge for viewing, reproducing, or downloading materials from their site can be held liable for copyright infringement if materials they make available are subject to another's copyright.

In 1998, Congress amended the copyright statute to provide liability limitations for some online material as a part of the Digital Millenium Copyright Act. The new section of 17 United States Code can be found in Appendix I. This new law exempts internet service providers from liability for materials found on the internet for which they are merely a passive conduit. Likewise, nonprofit educational institutions are, in some instances, relieved from liability for acts of infringement committed by faculty or graduate student employees engaged in teaching or research. The definitions in the statute should be reviewed carefully, since they determine who is exempt for what otherwise would be copyright infringement.

AVOIDING PROBLEMS ON THE INTERNET

As in most areas of life, the best course of action is to avoid legal entanglements whenever possible. Here are some suggestions to help you stay out of trouble on the internet.

- Conduct a federal, state, and common law search before adopting or registering a trademark, service mark, trade name, or domain name for use on the internet.

- Do not register or use famous trademarks of others as a domain name.

- When creating a website, carefully review all content accessible by the public. Use only content that is original, verifiably in the public domain, or for which you have the consent of the copyright owner.

- Make sure patent marking, copyright notices, and trademark notices are included as appropriate in the materials available to the public on your website. For example, if you wish to offer a product for sale that is protected by your U.S. patent, you may wish to footnote the product description to provide the conventional patent notice.

- Do not allow members of the public to upload material to your site. E-mail communication between site visitors and your webmaster are probably safe, however, since they are not usually accessible by the public.

- Do not offer for sale any products that might be subject to a claim of patent infringement. Staple products (which have many uses), products that have been on the market for more than about 20 years, and used products manufactured more than 20 years ago should be safe. Recently manufactured new, non-staple products can be offered at a minimal risk if purchased from a substantial supplier under a warranty of non-infringement.

- Do not defame any person or company that resides in a place where you do not want to be sued.

- If you have received a letter accusing you of infringement, or otherwise suspect that an intellectual property owner believes you are engaged in infringing activity, and the product alleged to be an infringement is not generally available, do not accept orders for that product from the owner's state if you want to avoid being sued there. For example, if the owner lives in New York, and you reside in California and sell your products directly to customers in California, Nevada, and Oregon, the owner may have to sue you in one of those three states unless he can establish "purposeful contacts" with New York. A sale to a customer in New York is often sufficient to establish jurisdiction of courts in New York over the infringement dispute. Needless to say, in such a circumstance the intellectual property owner often attempts to engineer such a sale to establish jurisdiction.

BIBLIOGRAPHY

"At Last, a Law to Catch the Chip Pirates." *Businessweek*, October 22, 1984, p. 39.

Becker, Stephen A. "Taking Care of Your Trademark." *PC Magazine*, February 21, 1984, pp. 473–474, 479–480.

Bunnin, Brad and Peter Beren. *Author Law & Strategies*, Nolo Press, 1983.

Burge, David A. *Patent and Trademark Tactics and Practice*, 2nd ed. John Wiley & Sons, Inc., 1984.

Burke, Alexander J., Jr. "Book Piracy: A Worldwide Threat to Authors and Publishers." *Imprint*, Spring 1985, pp. 4–5.

Code of Federal Regulations, Title 37.

Kaliski, Edward J. "Protecting Your Intellectual Property." *Mechanical Engineering*, January 1978, pp. 27–31.

Miller, Peggy A., Esq. "How the New Semiconductor Chip Protection Act Affects Your Company." *Computer Advertising News*, January 1985, pp. 12, 20.

"No Chips Off the Old Block." *Newsweek*, October 22, 1984, p. 80.

Ostrower, Donald A., Esq., P.E., and James Forster. "Protecting Against Unauthorized Reuse of Plans." *Consulting Engineer*, August 1980, pp. 16, 19–20.

Pooley, James. *Trade Secrets: How to Protect Your Ideas and Assets*, Osborne/McGraw-Hill, 1982.

Posch, Robert J., Jr. "Register Your Trademark and Protect the Image You're Selling." *Direct Marketing*, September 1983, pp. 116–120.

Ranney, Elizabeth. "Software Publishers Seek Patents." *InfoWorld*, September 1985, pp. 5–6.

Remer, Daniel. *Legal Care for Your Software*, Nolo Press, 1982, 1984.

Ross, Andrew, Esq. "Trade Secrets: What Are They and When Are They Protected?" *Engineering Perspective*, February 1983, p. 7.

Schwartz, Harry K., Esq., and Charles J. Hardy, Esq. "What the New Copyright Law Means to Engineers." *Professional Engineer*, June 1977, pp. 32–33.

United States Code, Title 35.

APPENDIX A
IMPORTANT ADDRESSES

Commissioner of Patents and Trademarks
Patent and Trademark Office
Washington, DC 20231
(703) 557-4636 (Automated Information Line)
(703) 557-4357 (Fees and General Information, Forms)
(703) 308-9617 (Attorneys Roster)
website:http://www.uspto.gov

This office supplies application forms for registering trademarks and information regarding trademarks and patents. General information, forms, and fees can be downloaded from the PTO website. In addition, access to a searchable database containing full-text U.S. patents issued since 1976 is available through this website.

Copyright Office
Information Section
Library of Congress
Washington, DC 20559
(202) 707-9100 if you know which forms you need
(202) 707-3000 if you do not know which forms you need
(Public Information)
website:http://www.lcweb.loc.gov

This office supplies information circulars and application forms for copyright registration. Specify the quantity and type of forms you need. They are free of charge. The office takes calls from 8:30 a.m. to 5 p.m., Eastern time, weekdays except holidays. You can leave a message on a recording machine any other time. You should receive the forms in about two weeks.

You can obtain up to five copies of the basic application forms from a local branch of the Copyright Office, if one is in your area. Alternatively, information, including current fees, and forms can be downloaded from the website shown above.

APPENDIX B
FEES AS OF JULY 1, 1999

Copyrights

Filing fee	$30
Renewal fee	45
Filing fee for mask works	75
Additional fee for expedited registration	500
Recording copyright assignments (one title)	50
Additional fee for 10 titles or fraction thereof	15

Patent[a]

Basic filing fee	$760
Each independent claim over three	78
Each claim of any type over 20	18
Additional fee for one or more multiple dependent claims	260
Design patent filing fee	310
Plant filing fee	480
Provisional application filing fee	150
Late submission of Information Disclosure Statement	240
Petitions (most)	130
Issue fee	1,210
Design patent issue fee	430
Plant patent issue fee	580
Maintenance fees	
for utility patents issued from applications filed before December 12, 1980	0
for utility patents issued from applications filed on or after December 12, 1980	
3 1/2 years from issuance	940
7 1/2 years from issuance	1,900
11 1/2 years from issuance	2,910
for design patents	0

[a] The small entity fee usually is half the amount shown.

Recording patent assignments, per document... 40
Copy of patent.. 3
Certificate of correction, patentee's error.. 100

Trademarks[b]
Application fee, for registration per class $245
Renewal fee, per class.. 300
Renewal fee after expiration date, per class... 400
Amendment to allege use/statement of use per case ITU application) 100
Appeal to Trademark Trial and Appeal Board, per class.............................. 100
Filing Section No. 8 affidavit, per class 100
Filing Section No. 15 affidavit, per class 100
Recording trademark assignment, agreement or other paper-per-mark
   per document.. 40

---

[b] There are no small entity rates for trademarks.

APPENDIX C
GLOSSARY OF TERMS

Author. In regard to copyrights, the legal owner of a literary work. Not necessarily the person who wrote the work.

Certification Mark. A mark used on the products, or in connection with the services, of someone other than the mark's owner, to certify the quality, accuracy, origin, material, manufacturing method, or other characteristics of the products or services.

Collective Mark. A mark used to indicate membership in a cooperative, association, or other collective organization.

Collective Membership Mark. A mark used to indicate membership in a union, association, or other organization.

Contributory Infringement. Selling items used to infringe a patent, knowingly in violation of the patent.

Copyright. Statutory protection granted to literary works. Gives owner the exclusive right to reproduce the work.

Corporate Opportunity Laws. Laws requiring employees to present potential money-making ideas to their employers before quitting to form their own company with the idea.

Direct Infringement. Producing or marketing a patented invention without the patent owner's permission.

Discovery. A period preceding a patent, trademark, or copyright infringement, trade secret, or other trial during which each side collects from the other documents that might relate to the case.

Fair Use. Certain uses of copyrightable material that do not constitute infringement, e.g., criticism, comment, news reporting, teaching, scholarship, or research.

Fictitious Name. A commercially used name that does not fully identify the user.

Fixed and Tangible Form. In permanent, tangible form, e.g., in print or on a recording.

Inducement of Infringement. Encouraging or aiding another person to infringe a patent.

Intellectual Property. Certain creative works, e.g., original literature, computer software, trademarks, trade secrets, semiconductor chip masks, and inventions.

Invention. A novel and useful idea that has been reduced to practice.

Jepson-Type Format. A format for claims on a patent application, containing a description of a particular invention's known elements, a transition phrase, and the new elements.

Means Plus Function Format. Patent application claim format that expresses a means or step by which a particular invention performs a specified function without having to describe the structure, material, or acts required to perform the function.

Nonobviousness. Would not have been obvious to someone with ordinary skill in a particular invention's field.

Notice of Allowance. A notice sent by the Patent and Trademark Office signifying that the examiner has approved a patent application.

Office Action. An action taken by the Patent and Trademark Office that requires a response from the applicant.

Patent. A deed to a particular invention.

Preliminary Injunction. A court order that forbids a defendant from making, using, or selling something, or from engaging in specific activities, until a full trial can be held.

Principal Register. One of two federal registers of trademarks and other marks. Marks on this register carry the presumption of validity.

Prior Art. Previous contributions to the technology that a new invention advances.

Product by Process. Patent claims that define the steps for producing a particular product.

Prosecution Period. Period between the date the Patent and Trademark Office receives a patent application and the date the patent is granted or the application abandoned.

Public Domain. Works that belong to the public and, therefore, are unprotectable by any individual.

Publication. The distribution of copies of a work to the public by sale or other transfer of ownership, or by rental, lease, or lending.

Service Mark. A mark used by a business in selling or advertising its services to distinguish them from its competitors' services.

Small Entity Status. Status as a sole inventor, joint inventors, a nonprofit organization, or a business with 500 or fewer employees, which enables the entity to reduce many patent fees by 50 percent.

Supplemental Register. One of two federal registers of trademarks and other marks. Marks on this register do not carry the presumption of validity.

Temporary Restraining Order (TRO). A court order that temporarily stops a person or company from engaging in a particular activity until an emergency hearing can be conducted. A TRO may be converted to a preliminary injunction following a hearing.

Trade Name. The name by which the public knows a particular business.

Trade Secret. Secret information that gives a business an advantage over competitors who do not have the information.

Trademark. A word, name, or symbol that a business uses to distinguish its products or services from those of its competitors.

Work-Made-For-Hire. A work typically created by an employee as part of his job. A work-made-for-hire belongs to employer, who is recognized as legal author and copyright owner.

Writ of Attachment. A court order that prevents a lawsuit defendant from moving his funds or other assets until the trial concludes.

APPENDIX D

SAMPLE NONDISCLOSURE AGREEMENT

This agreement is between _____("OWNER") and_____("RECIPIENT"). Whereas OWNER possesses certain confidential information relating to _____
_____ *(a)*
("INFORMATION"); and whereas RECIPIENT wishes to evaluate such information to determine if a beneficial business relationship between the parties relating to the use of the INFORMATION would be in the best interests of both parties; NOW THEREFORE, in consideration of OWNER's agreement to furnish such information, RECIPIENT agrees to receive the INFORMATION under the following terms.

1. RECIPIENT agrees to receive and maintain any INFORMATION provided pursuant to this Agreement, whether in written, oral, visual, or tangible form such as models or samples, in strict confidence. RECIPIENT agrees to take reasonable precautions to prevent disclosure of OWNER's INFORMATION to any third person.

2. RECIPIENT agrees not to use OWNER's INFORMATION for his/her/its own benefit, or for the benefit of any person or entity, other than OWNER, except as provided in any subsequent written agreement between OWNER and RECIPIENT.

(a) For example, information relating to manufacturing, engineering, production, storage and/or sales activities of OWNER or new technologies being developed by OWNER, including but not limited to data, marketing and advertising plans, computer programs, customer, client and vendor identities and records, and other information pertaining to the performance, plans, strategies, and other business of the OWNER, that is proprietary, confidential, and/or trade secret information of OWNER. (Note: Try to be as specific as possible in defining the kind of information or technology that is being disclosed under the agreement.)

3. RECIPIENT agrees to return to OWNER upon request all tangible and written INFORMATION furnished under this agreement and any copies of the same that may have been made by RECIPIENT.

4. RECIPIENT's obligations under this agreement shall not apply to any INFORMATION that: was known to RECIPIENT before any disclosure was made by OWNER; is now or hereafter becomes known to the public through no breach of this agreement; or, becomes known to RECIPIENT, by a disclosure from a person or organization, other than OWNER, having no obligation to either OWNER or RECIPIENT to maintain the INFORMATION in confidence.

RECIPIENT:

_____
SIGNATURE

_____   _____
PRINTED NAME/TITLE   DATE

APPENDIX E

EMPLOYEE/INDEPENDENT CONTRACTOR ASSIGNMENT AND CONFIDENTIALITY AGREEMENT

In consideration for his or her employment by _____ (the "COMPANY"), _____ (the "WORKER") agrees as follows:

The WORKER understands that during the course of employment with the COMPANY, the WORKER may receive confidential information and trade secrets of the COMPANY, and may be asked to create, improve, write, edit, review, alter, upgrade, modify, or otherwise handle or process reports, booklets, books, manuals, other documents, illustrations, tables of data, photographs, shop drawings, blueprints, computer programs, inventions or other devices, packaging, trademarks, service marks, trade names, and promotional materials and similar works that may contain or be considered confidential or trade secret material and that have or may have value.

The WORKER agrees not to disclose to others outside the COMPANY, or to use for his or her benefit or for the benefit of any person or entity other than the COMPANY, any information received from the COMPANY, unless such information is known to the public at the time the WORKER began his or her employment or subsequently becomes known to the public through no fault of the WORKER.

The WORKER hereby expressly agrees to assign and convey all rights, title, and interest of all types whatsoever in connection with his or her work to the COMPANY, including but not limited to copyrights, trademarks, service marks, patent rights, publicity rights, publication rights, marketing rights, and distribution rights, and rights regarding titling, authors' names, right to create derivative works, and the size and color of finished works. The parties intend that this agreement to assign shall be valid regardless of whether the WORKER is determined to be an employee of the COMPANY, an independent contractor, or an agent, officer, or director of the COMPANY.

The WORKER agrees and warrants that any works produced by the WORKER for the COMPANY and not identified by the WORKER as coming from another source shall be the original work of the WORKER and not subject to a claim of ownership by any third person. The WORKER agrees to attach to this agreement a disclosure of all works created before his or her employment with the COMPANY in which the WORKER claims ownership.[a]

The WORKER agrees that the sole consideration given for the WORKER's assignment of rights and obligation of confidentiality shall be the WORKER's salary, whether made on an hourly, biweekly, monthly, lump-sum, per-unit, or other basis.

RECIPIENT:

_____
SIGNATURE

_____   _____
PRINTED NAME/TITLE   DATE

---

[a] California employers should include the following notice after the last sentence in this clause:

California Labor Code Section 2870 provides that this assignment shall not apply to any invention that the employee develops entirely on his or her own time without using the employer's equipment, supplies, facilities, or trade secret information, unless such inventions relate, at the time of conception or reduction, to practice of the invention, to the employer's business, or actual or demonstrably anticipated research or development of the employer, or the inventions result from any work performed by the employee for the employer.

PROFESSIONAL PUBLICATIONS, INC.

APPENDIX F
SAMPLE NONCOMPETITION AGREEMENT

In consideration for his or her employment by _____
_____ (the "COMPANY"),
_____ (the "EMPLOYEE"),
agrees as follows:

The EMPLOYEE agrees not to compete with the COMPANY in its current or projected areas of specialization, which include but are not limited to, _____
_____

(a)

and any other business that the COMPANY may enter or engage in during the term of EMPLOYEE's employment (the "COMPANY's BUSINESS"), for a period of_____ (b)
years in the _____ (c)
after the termination of EMPLOYEE's employment with COMPANY. Competition includes the giving of advice or counsel to others, whether with or without fee, or developing, marketing, or selling products or services that relate to the COMPANY's BUSINESS.

(a) The identification of the COMPANY's current and projected business should be detailed to increase the agreement's chance of enforceability.

(b) The noncompetition period should be as short as possible. No more than five years is recommended. If the geographical area is very large (i.e., an entire state or all of the United States), the time period should be much less than five years, perhaps only one or two years. If the geographical area is rather limited (e.g., a city or county), a court is more likely to enforce a longer period of noncompetition like five years.

(c) This blank is for the geographical area of noncompetition. The area should bear some relation to the business of the COMPANY. If the COMPANY does business throughout the U.S., it would be proper to use the U.S. as the geographical area of noncompetition. Keep in mind, however, that courts do not like to enforce noncompetition agreements, and will only enforce those that are reasonable as to geographical area and time.

EMPLOYEE:

_____

SIGNATURE

_____   _____

PRINTED NAME/TITLE   DATE

APPENDIX G
SAMPLE EXPRESS MAIL CERTIFICATE OF MAILING

I hereby certify that this correspondence is being deposited with the United States Postal Service "Express Mail Service" Label No. _____ , postage paid, in an envelope addressed to: Commissioner of Patents and Trademarks, Washington, D.C. 20231 on _____ .

DATE

DATED: _____ BY:_____

APPENDIX H
PCT COUNTRIES/REGIONS AS OF MAY 1999

In the Americas

Barbados	BB
Brazil	BR
Canada	CA
Cuba	CU
Grenada	GD
Mexico	MX
Saint Lucia	LC
Trinidad & Tobago	TT
United States	US

In Africa

ARIPO (AP)

Gambia	GM
Ghana	GH
Kenya	KE
Lesotho	LS
Malawi	MW
Sudan	SD
Swaziland*	SZ
Uganda	UG
Zimbabwe	ZW

OAPI (OA)

Burkina Faso*	BF
Benin*	BJ
Central African Republic*	CF
Chad*	TD
Congo*	CG

Cote d'Ivoire*	CI
Cameroon*	CM
Gabon*	GA
Guinea*	GN
Guinea-Bissau*	GW
Mali*	ML
Mauretania*	MR
Niger*	NE
Senegal*	SN
Togo*	TG

Non-ARIPO or OAPI

Liberia	LR
Sierra Leone	SL
South Africa	ZA

In Europe

EPC

Austria	AT
Belgium*	BE
Cyprus*	CY
Denmark	DK
Finland	FI
France*	FR
Germany	DE
Great Britain	GB
Greece*	GR
Ireland*	IE
Italy*	IT

---

*May only be designated as a regional patent ("national" route via the PCT has been closed)

Lichtenstein	LI
Luxembourg	LU
Monaco*	MC
Netherlands*	NL
Portugal	PL
Spain	ES
Sweden	SE
Switzerland	CH

Non-EPC

Albania	AL
Bulgaria	BG
Bosnia & Hertzegovina	BA
Belarus	BY
Croatia	HR
Czech Republic	CZ
Estonia	EE
Hungary	HU
Iceland	IS
Lithuania	LT
Latvia	LV
Republic of Moldova	MD
Former Yugoslav Republic of Macedonia	MK
Norway	NO
Poland	PL
Romania	RO

In Asia and the Pacific

Armenia	AM
Australia	AU
Azerbaijan	AZ
China	CN
Georgia	GE
India	IN
Indonesia	ID
Israel	IL
Japan	JP
Kyrgyzstan	KG
Korea (PRK)	KP
Republic of Korea	KR
Kazakhstan	KZ
Sri Lanka	LK
Mongolia	MN
New Zealand	NZ
Singapore	SG
Tajikistan	TJ
Turkmenistan	TM
Uzbekistan	UZ
Vietnam	VN

*May only be designated as a regional patent ("national" route via the PCT has been closed)

APPENDIX I
LIMITATIONS ON LIABILITY RELATING TO
MATERIALS ONLINE (17 USC §512)

(a) **Transitory Digital Network Communications.** A service provider shall not be liable for monetary relief, or, except as provided in subsection (j), for injunctive or other equitable relief, for infringement of copyright by reason of the provider's transmitting, routing, or providing connections for material through a system or network controlled or operated by or for the service provider, or by reason of the intermediate and transient storage of that material in the course or such transmitting, routing, or providing connections, if

(1) the transmission of the material was initiated by or at the direction of a person other than the service provider;

(2) the transmission, routing provision of connections, or storage is carried out through an automatic technical process without selection of the material by the service provider;

(3) the service provider does not select the recipients of the material except as an automatic response to the request of another person;

(4) no copy of the material made by the service provider in the course of such intermediate or transient storage is maintained on the system or network in a manner ordinarily accessible to anyone other than anticipated recipients, and no such copy is maintained on the system or network in a manner ordinarily accessible to such anticipated recipients for a longer period than is reasonably necessary for the transmission, routing, and provision of connections; and

(5) the material is transmitted through the system or network without modification of its content.

(b) **System Caching.**

(1) *Limitation of liability.* A service provider shall not be liable for monetary relief, or, except as provided in subsection (j), for injunctive or other equitable relief, for infringement of copyright by reason of the intermediate

and temporary storage of material on a system or network controlled or operated by or for the service provider in a case in which

(A) the material is made available online by a person other than the service provider;

(B) the material is transmitted from the person described in subparagraph (A) through the system or network to a person other than the person described in subparagraph (A) at the direction of that other person; and

(C) the storage is carried out through an automatic technical process for the purpose of making the material available to users of the system or network who, after the material is transmitted as described in subparagraph (B), request access to the material from the person described in subparagraph (A), if the conditions set forth in paragraph (2) are met.

(2) *Conditions.* The conditions referred to in paragraph (1) are that

(A) the material described in paragraph (1) is transmitted to the subsequent users described in paragraph (1)(C) without modification to its content from the manner in which the material was transmitted from the person described in paragraph (1)(A);

(B) the service provider described in paragraph (1) complies with rules concerning the refreshing, reloading, or other updating of the material when specified by the person making the material available online in accordance with a generally accepted industry standard data communications protocol for the system or network through which that person makes the material available, except that this subparagraph applies only if those rules are not used by the person described in paragraph (1)(A) to prevent or unreasonably impair the intermediate storage to which this subsection applies;

(C) the service provider does not interfere with the ability of technology associated with the material to return to the person described in paragraph (1)(A) the information that would have been available to that person if the material had been obtained by the subsequent users described in paragraph (1)(C) directly from that person, except that this subparagraph applies only if that technology

(i) does not significantly interfere with the performance of the provider's system or network or with the intermediate storage of the material;

(ii) is consistent with generally accepted industry standard communications protocols; and

(iii) does not extract information from the provider's system or network other than the information that would have been available to the person described in paragraph (1)(A) if the subsequent users had gained access to the material directly from the person;

(D) if the person described in paragraph (1)(A) has in effect a condition that a person must meet prior to having access to the material, such as a condition based on payment of a fee or provision of a password or other information, the service provider permits access to the stored material in significant part only to users of its system or network that have met those conditions and only in accordance with those conditions; and

(E) if the person described in paragraph (1)(A) makes that material available online without the authorization of the copyright owner of the material, the service provider responds expeditiously to remove, or disable access to, the material that is claimed to be infringing upon notification of claimed infringement as described in subsection (c)(3), except that this subparagraph applies only if

(i) the material has previously been removed from the originating site or access to it has been disabled, or a court has ordered that the material be removed from the originating site or that access to the material on the originating site be disabled; and

(ii) the party giving the notification includes in the notification a statement confirming that the material has been removed from the originating site or access to it has been disabled or that a court has ordered that the material be removed from the originating site or that access to the material on the originating site be disabled.

(c) **Information Residing on Systems or Networks at Direction of Users.**

(1) *In general.* A service provider shall not be liable for monetary relief, or, except as provided in subsection (j), for injunctive or other equitable relief, for infringement of copyright by reason of the storage at the direction of a user or material that resides on a system or network controlled or operated by or for the service provider, if the service provider

(A) (i) does not have actual knowledge that the material or an activity using the material on the system or network is infringing;

(ii) in the absence of such actual knowledge, is not aware of facts or circumstances from which infringing activity is apparent; or

(iii) upon obtaining such knowledge or awareness, acts expeditiously to remove, or disable access to, the material;

(B) does not receive a financial benefit directly attributable to the infringing activity, in a case in which the service provider has the right and ability to control such activity; and

(C) upon notification of claimed infringement as described in paragraph (3), responds expeditiously to remove, or disable access to, the material that is claimed to be infringing or to be the subject of infringing activity.

(2) *Designated agent.* The limitations on liability established in this subsection apply to a service provider only if the service provider has designated an agent to receive notifications of claimed infringement described in paragraph (3), by making available through its service, including on its website in a location accessible to the public, and by providing to the Copyright Office, substantially the following information:

(A) the name, address, phone number, and electronic mail address of the agent.

(B) other contact information which the Register of Copyrights may deem appropriate. The Register of Copyrights shall maintain a current directory of agents available to the public for inspection, including through the Internet, in both electronic and hard copy formats and may require payment of a fee by service providers to cover the costs of maintaining the directory.

(3) *Elements of notification.*

(A) To be effective under this subsection, a notification of claimed infringement must be a written communication provided to the designated agent of a service provider that includes substantially the following;

(i) A physical or electronic signature of a person authorized to act on behalf of the owner of an exclusive right that is allegedly infringed.

(ii) Identification of the copyrighted work claimed to have been infringed, or, if multiple copyrighted works at a single online site are covered by a single notification, a representative list of such works at that site.

(iii) Identification of the material that is claimed to be infringing or to be the subject of infringing activity and that is to be removed or access to which is to be disabled, and information reasonably sufficient to permit the service provider to locate the material.

(iv) Information reasonably sufficient to permit the service provider to contact the complaining party, such as an address, telephone number, and, if available, an electronic mail address at which the complaining party may be contacted.

(v) A statement that the complaining party has a good faith belief that use of the material in the manner complained of is not authorized by the copyright owner, its agent, or the law.

(vi) A statement that the information in the notification is accurate, and under penalty of perjury, that the complaining party is authorized to act on behalf of the owner of an exclusive right that is allegedly infringed.

(B) (i) Subject to clause (ii), a notification from a copyright owner or from a person authorized to act on behalf of the copyright owner that fails to comply substantially with the provisions of subparagraph (A) shall not be considered under paragraph (1)(A) in determining whether a service provider has actual knowledge or is aware of facts or circumstances from which infringing activity is apparent.

(ii) In a case in which the notification that is provided to the service provider's designated agent fails to comply substantially with all the provisions of subparagraph (A) but substantially complies with clauses (ii), (iii), and (iv) of subparagraph (A), clause (i) of this subparagraph applies only if the service provider promptly attempts to contact the person making the notification or takes other reasonable steps to assist in the receipt of notification that substantially complies with all the provisions of subparagraph (A).

(d) **Information Location Tools.** A service provider shall not be liable for monetary relief, or, except as provided in subsection (j), for injunctive or other equitable relief, for infringement of copyright by reason of the provider referring or linking users to an online location containing infringing material or infringing activity, by using information location tools, including a directory, index, reference, pointer or hypertext link, if the service provider

(1) (A) does not have actual knowledge that the material or activity is infringing;

(B) in the absence of such actual knowledge, is not aware of facts or circumstances from which infringing activity is apparent; or

(C) upon obtaining such knowledge or awareness, acts expeditiously to remove, or disable access to, the material;

(2) does not receive a financial benefit directly attributable to the infringing activity, in a case in which the service provider has the right and ability to control such activity; and

(3) upon notification of claimed infringement as described in subsection (c)(3), responds expeditiously to remove, or disable access to, the material that is claimed to be infringing or to be the subject of infringing activity, except that, for purposes of this paragraph, the information described in subsection (c)(3)(A)(iii) shall be identification of the reference or link, to material or activity claimed to be infringing, that is to be removed or access to which is to be disabled, and information reasonably sufficient to permit the service provider to locate the reference or link.

(e) **Limitation on liability of nonprofit educational institutions.**

(1) When a public or other nonprofit institution of higher education is a service provider, and when a faculty member or graduate student who is an employee of such institution is performing a teaching or research function, for the purposes of subsections (a) and (b), such faculty member or graduate student shall be considered to be a person other than the institution, and for the purposes of subsections (c) and (d), such faculty member's or graduate student's knowledge of awareness of his or her infringing activities shall not be attributed to the institution, if

(A) such faculty member's or graduate student's infringing activities do not involve the provision of online access to instructional materials that are or were required or recommended within the preceding 3-year period, for a course taught at the institution by such faculty member of graduate student;

(B) the institution has not, within the preceding 3-year period, received more than two notifications described in subsection (c)(3) of claimed infringement and such notifications of claimed infringement were not actionable under subsection (f); and

(C) the institution provides to all users of its system or network informational materials that accurately describe, and promote compliance with, the laws of the United States relating to copyright.

(2) *Injunctions.* For the purposes of this subsection, the limitations on injunctive relief contained in subsections (j)(2) and (j)(3), but not those in (j)(1), shall apply.

(f) **Misrepresentations.** Any person who knowingly materially misrepresents under this section

(1) the material or activity is infringing, or

(2) that material or activity was removed or disabled by mistake or misidentification, shall be liable for any damages, including costs and attorneys' fees, incurred by the alleged infringer, by any copyright owner or copyright owner's authorized licensee, or by a service provider, who is injured by such misrepresentations, as the result of the service provider relying upon such misrepresentation in removing or disabling access to the material or activity claimed to be infringing, or in replacing the removed material or ceasing to disable access to it.

(g) **Replacement of Removed or Disabled Material and Limitation on Other Liability.**

(1) *No liability for taking down generally.* Subject to paragraph (2), a service provider shall not be liable to any person for any claim based on the service provider's good faith disabling of access to, or removal of, material or activity claimed to be infringing or based on facts or circumstances from which infringing activity is apparent, regardless of whether the material or activity is ultimately determined to be infringing.

(2) *Exception.* Paragraph (1) shall not apply with respect to material residing at the direction of a subscriber of the service provider on a system or network controlled or operated by or for the service provider that is removed, or to which access is disabled by the service provider, pursuant to a notice provided under subsection (c)(1)(C), unless the service provider

(A) takes reasonable steps promptly to notify the subscriber that it has removed or disabled access to the material;

(B) upon receipt of a counter notification described in paragraph (3), promptly provides the person who provided the notification under subsection (c)(1)(C) with a copy of the counter notification, and informs that person that it will replace the removed material or cease disabling access to it in 10 business days; and

(C) replaces the removed material and ceases disabling access to it not less than 10, nor more than 14, business days following receipt of the counter notice, unless its designated agent first receives notice from the person who submitted the notification under subsection (c)(1)(C) that such person has filed an action seeking a court order to restrain the subscriber from engaging in infringing activity relating to the material on the service provider's system or network.

(3) *Contents of counter notification.* To be effective under this subsection, a counter notification must be a written communication provided to the service provider's designated agent that includes substantially the following:

(A) A physical or electronic signature of the subscriber.

(B) Identification of the material that has been removed or to which access has been disabled and the location at which the material appeared before it was removed or access to it was disabled.

(C) a statement under penalty of perjury that the subscriber has a good faith belief that the material was removed or disabled as a result of mistake or misidentification of the material to be removed or disabled.

(D) The subscriber's name, address, and telephone number, and a statement that the subscriber consents to the jurisdiction of Federal District Court for the judicial district in which the address is located, or if the subscriber's address is outside of the United States, for any judicial district in which the service provider may be found, and that the subscriber will accept service of process from the person who provided notification under subsection (c)(1)(C) or an agent of such person.

(4) *Limitation on other liability.* A service provider's compliance with paragraph (2) shall not subject the service provider to liability for copyright infringement with respect to the material identified in the notice provided under subsection (c)(1)(C).

(h) **Subpoena to Identify Infringer.**

(1) *Request.* A copyright owner or a person authorized to act on the owner's behalf may request the clerk of any United States district court to issue a subpoena to a service provider for identification of an alleged infringer in accordance with this subsection.

(2) *Contents of request.* The request may be made by filing with the clerk

(A) a copy of a notification described in subsection (c)(3)(A);

(B) a proposed subpoena; and

(C) a sworn declaration to the effect that the purpose for which the subpoena is sought is to obtain the identity of an alleged infringer and that such information will only be used for the purpose of protecting rights under this title.

(3) *Contents of subpoena.* The subpoena shall authorize and order the service provider receiving the notification and the subpoena to expeditiously disclose to the copyright owner or person authorized by the copyright owner information sufficient to identify the alleged infringer of the material described in the notification to the extent such information is available to the service provider.

(4) *Basis for granting subpoena.* If the notification filed satisfies the provisions of subsection (c)(3)(A), the proposed subpoena is in proper form, and the accompanying declaration is properly executed, the clerk shall expeditiously issue and sign the proposed subpoena and return it to the requester for delivery to the service provider.

(5) *Actions of service provider receiving subpoena.* Upon receipt of the issued subpoena, either accompanying or subsequent to the receipt of a notification described in subsection (c)(3)(A), the service provider shall expeditiously disclose to the copyright owner or person authorized by the copyright owner the information required by the subpoena, notwithstanding any other provision of law and regardless of whether the service provider responds to the notification.

(6) *Rules applicable to subpoena.* Unless otherwise provided by this section or by applicable rules of the court, the procedure for issuance and delivery of the subpoena, and the remedies for noncompliance with the subpoena, shall be governed to the greatest extent practicable by those provisions of the Federal Rules of Civil Procedure governing the issuance, service, and enforcement of a subpoena duces tecum.

(i) **Conditions for Eligibility.**

(1) *Accommodation of technology.* The limitations on liability established by this section shall apply to a service provider only if the service provider

(A) has adopted and reasonably implemented, and informs subscribers and account holders of the service provider's system or network of, a policy that provides for the termination in appropriate circumstances of subscribers and account holders of the service providers system or network who are repeat infringers; and

(B) accommodates and does not interfere with standard technical measures.

(2) *Definition.* As used in this subsection, the term "standard technical measures" means technical measures that are used by copyright owners to identify or protect copyrighted works and

(A) have been developed pursuant to a broad consensus of copyright owners and service providers in an open, fair, voluntary, multi-industry standards process;

(B) are available to any person on reasonable and nondiscriminatory terms; and

(C) do not impose substantial costs on service providers or substantial burdens on their systems or networks.

(j) **Injunctions.** The following rules shall apply in the case of any application for an injunction under section 502 against a service provider that is not subject to monetary remedies under this section:

(1) *Scope of relief.*

(A) With respect to conduct other than that which qualifies for the limitation on remedies set forth in subsection (a), the court may grant injunctive relief with respect to a service provider only in one or more of the following forms:

(i) An order restraining the service provider from providing access to infringing material or activity residing at a particular online site on the provider's system or network.

(ii) An order restraining the service provider from providing access to a subscriber or account holder of the service provider's system or network who is engaging in infringing activity and is identified in the order, by terminating the accounts of the subscriber or account holder that are specified in the order.

(iii) Such other injunctive relief as the court may consider necessary to prevent or restrain infringement of copyrighted materials specified in the order of the court at a particular online location, if such relief is the least burdensome to the service provider among the forms of relief comparably effective for that purpose.

(B) If the service provider qualifies for the limitation on remedies described in subsection (a), the court may only grant injunctive relief in one or both of the following forms:

(i) An order restraining the service provider from providing access to a subscriber or account holder of the service provider's system or network who is using the provider's service to engage in infringing activity and is identified in the order, by terminating the accounts of the subscriber or account holder that are specified in the order.

(ii) An order restraining the service provider from providing access, by taking reasonable steps specified in the order to block access to a specific, identified, online location outside the United States.

(2) *Considerations.* The court, in considering the relevant criteria for injunctive relief under applicable law, shall consider

(A) whether such an injunction, either alone or in combination with other such injunctions issued against the same service provider under this subsection, would significantly burden either the provider or the operation of the provider's system or network;

(B) the magnitude of the harm likely to be suffered by the copyright owner in the digital network environment if steps are not taken to prevent or restrain the infringement;

(C) whether implementation of such an injunction would be technically feasible and effective, and would not interfere with access to noninfringing material at other online locations; and

(D) whether other less burdensome and comparably effective means of preventing or restraining access to the infringing material are available.

(3) *Notice and ex parte orders.* Injunctive relief under this subsection shall be available only after notice to the service provider and an opportunity for the service provider to appear are provided, except for orders ensuring the preservation of evidence or other orders having no material adverse effect on the operation of the service provider's communications network.

(k) **Definitions.**

(1) *Service provider.*

(A) As used in subsection (a), the term "service provider" means an entity offering the transmission, routing, or providing of connections for digital online communications, between or among points specified by a user, or material of the user's choosing, without modification to the content of the material as sent or received.

(B) As used in this section, other than subsection (a), the term "service provider" means a provider of online services or network access, or the operator of facilities therefore, and includes an entity described in subparagraph (A).

(2) *Monetary relief.* As used in this section, the term "monetary relief" means damages, costs, attorneys' fees, and any other form of monetary payment.

(l) **Other Defenses Not Affected.** The failure of a service provider's conduct to qualify for limitation of liability under this section shall not bear adversely upon the consideration of a defense by the service provider that the service provider's conduct is not infringing under this title or any other defense.

(m) **Protection of Privacy.** Nothing in this section shall be construed to condition the applicability of subsections (a) through (d) on

(1) a service provider monitoring its service or affirmatively seeking facts indicating infringing activity, except to the extent consistent with a standard technical measure complying with the provisions of subsection (i); or

(2) a service provider gaining access to, removing, or disabling access to material in cases in which such conduct is prohibited by law.

(n) **Construction.** Subsections (a), (b), (c), and (d) describe separate and distinct functions for purposes of applying this section. Whether a service provider qualifies for the limitation on liability in any one of those subsections shall be based solely on the criteria in that subsection, and shall not affect a determination of whether that service provider qualifies for the limitations on liability under any other such subsection.

Leg.H. October 28, 1998, P.L. 105-304 §202, 112 Stat. 2877.

INDEX

©
book piracy, 16–17
foreign protection, 11, 11 (ftn), 14
semiconductor chips, 23–24
software, 20
written works, 10–12
Ⓜ, 23–24
Ⓟ, 11
®, 52
™, 51–52

A
abandoned marks, 49
addresses for relevant offices, 65
allowance, 31
"All rights reserved," 11, 11 (ftn), 14
Anonymous in copyrights, 11
appeals of patent rejection, 31
application review for patents, 30–31
arbitrary marks, 48, 51
attorneys (*see* lawyers)
audiotapes and copyrights, 1
audiovisual works and copyrights, 9

B
Berne Convention, 13–14
book piracy and copyrights, 16–17
broadening reissue in patent application, 32
Buenos Aires Convention (BAC), 14
burden of proof for copyright infringements, 14–15

C
California trade secrets laws, 39
certificate of correction petition, 32
certificate of mailing, 28, 79
certification marks, 47, 69

Chip Act (*see* Semiconductor Chip Protection Act)
coined marks, 47, 51
collaborative registration in copyrights, 11
collective marks, 47, 69
common law, 39 (ftn)
computer software (*see* software)
confidentiality pledge
sample contract, 75–76
trade secrets, 41–42
Constitution, U.S., and intellectual property laws, 2
Copyright Acts (1976, 1989), 6–7
Copyright Clearance Center, 16
Copyright Office, U.S., 4, 65
copyrights
address for Copyright Office, 65
claiming, 3–4
engineering works, 17–18
error correction, 6
fair use, 15–16, 69
fees, 67
foreign protection, 11, 11 (ftn), 14
infringement of, 14–17
Internet, 59–60
legislation, 6–7, 22, 60
notice symbol and format
international protection, 11, 11 (ftn)
semiconductor chips, 23–24
software, 20
written works, 10–12
protection jurisdiction, 13–14
registration, 4–6
advantages to, 12–13
expedited, 5–6
misconceptions, 9

PROFESSIONAL PUBLICATIONS, INC.